INTRODUCTION

FROM THE

Chairman of Burrell Renaissance

Sir William Burrell left his mark on the world, both as a highly successful businessman and as an international art collector and philanthropist. His gift to the people of Glasgow cannot be underestimated. And as we work on the refurbishment and redisplay of the Burrell Collection building, we also have the opportunity to fully realize the collection's potential on a global stage.

Sir William devoted more than 75 years of his life to amassing one of the world's greatest, single personal collections. The Burrell Collection is of world-class quality, and reflects the outward-looking, international confidence of a very great collector. It tells us much about the ambitious and wide-ranging context in which Sir William Burrell and Glasgow flourished in his time. It also has current relevance to understanding Scottish aspirations. Burrell's high standards and astuteness were matched by his competitive reach and his energetic persistence.

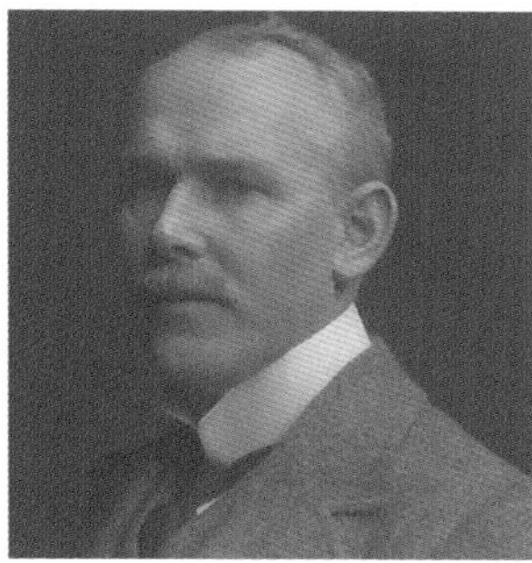

William Burrell, c.1920

Burrell's gift is an international flagship for Glasgow – and I am delighted that we are able to display some of its treasures in Kelvingrove while the renaissance of the Burrell Collection takes place. These works are the medieval highlights from an outstanding collection of more than 9,000 objects, and we are grateful to have had the assistance of a contemporary collector in co-curating this display – Sir Paul Ruddock, whose passion for medieval objects perhaps equals Sir William's.

Much has moved on since the initial priority of creating a home for the collection. The current renaissance of the Burrell Collection will place the true significance of Sir William's legacy within the international league where it should be set. The challenge is highly ambitious, but what a privilege it is for our generation to be asked to rise to that call and to take forward this great inheritance. And we are fortunate to be able to test new approaches to displays in the splendid surroundings of another of Glasgow's best-loved buildings, Kelvingrove Art Gallery and Museum.

Glasgow has been defined by international aspirations and cultural reach. Sir William entrusted his life's work to the city he called home. Mindful always of his wishes, we are seeking to secure much wider recognition of his vision and achievements. I believe that our high ambitions for the Burrell Collection will take forward the torch handed to us and place his extraordinary collection within the international context which it deserves.

Sir Angus Grossart

CHAIRMAN

Burrell Renaissance

THE BURRELL AT KELVINGROVE
Collecting Medieval Treasures

by Sir Paul Ruddock, Former Chairman of the Victoria and Albert Museum, London

Sir William Burrell (1861–1958) was a major Scottish ship-owner who gifted his collection to the City of Glasgow in 1944. It principally covers European paintings, particularly French nineteenth-century art; Egyptian, Greek, Roman and Near Eastern art; Chinese ceramics, bronzes and jades; Islamic art, especially textiles; European arms and armour and decorative art. One of the undoubted highlights, however, is the medieval European collection. I have had a passion for the Middle Ages for the last 50 years, and so when James Robinson, Director of the Burrell Renaissance, asked me to curate an exhibition of medieval objects from the Burrell I jumped at the opportunity.

The nation waited with bated breath for the opening in 1983 of the purpose-built Burrell Collection museum designed by Barry Gasson, John Meunier and Brit Andresen in the verdant surroundings of Pollok Country Park on the south side of Glasgow. After welcoming more than 12 million visitors in over 30 years, the museum is now closed for a comprehensive renovation, and the current exhibition is the first of a series planned at Kelvingrove Art Gallery and Museum that will showcase between 2018 and 2020 the Collection's highlights.

In the late Middle Ages (c.1100–1500 AD), works of art were mainly commissioned by the Church for the glory of God. Nobles and wealthy burghers also commissioned artists to furnish their homes or to provide gifts to their local cathedral or monastery. The artists and craftsmen of this period were, for the most part, anonymous, but their skills were every bit as great as their Renaissance successors. My own fascination with this period began with childhood visits to National Trust houses and medieval cathedrals where I fell in love with the incredible beauty of Romanesque and Gothic art.

Today, the art of the Middle Ages is completely out of fashion and I may be one of only a handful of people who have been collecting in this area over the past 30 years. However, in the late nineteenth and early twentieth century, medieval art had the popularity amongst wealthy collectors that contemporary art has today. This was the period of the great Gothic revival that shaped the civic identity of many British cities, such as Birmingham and Manchester. Pre-Raphaelite painters courted controversy and achieved great notoriety as they consciously sought inspiration from the medieval past, rejecting the classical order of the Renaissance. Designers and architects such as AWN Pugin and William Morris flourished in an age that also saw Roman Catholic emancipation and a renewed fascination with the religious practices that had been largely excised by the Reformation in the sixteenth century. Across the Atlantic, American tycoons such as John Pierpoint Morgan, Henry Walters, Henry Clay Frick and William Randolph Hearst were battling each other to buy the best medieval tapestries, stained glass and sculpture to ornament their baronial mansions, while newly wealthy businessmen were furnishing their homes in a style that they believed enhanced their status by mirroring the stately homes of old.

Burrell started collecting avidly in the 1890s but it is only from 1911 that detailed records of his purchases survive. Much of what is presented in the current exhibition was acquired for Hutton Castle in the Scottish Borders, which he bought in 1916. However, due to extensive building works it was not until 1927 that he and his family could take up residence. This period also coincides with a ramp-up in his expenditure on acquisitions. Until 1915 he spent about £500 a year on his collection, but from 1911–1957 his expenditure averaged £20,000 a year (about £1 million in today's money) and there were peak years of £80,000 in 1936 and £60,000 in 1948. These were enormous sums in Britain for the Depression years of the 1930s and the immediate post-war austerity of the late 1940s.

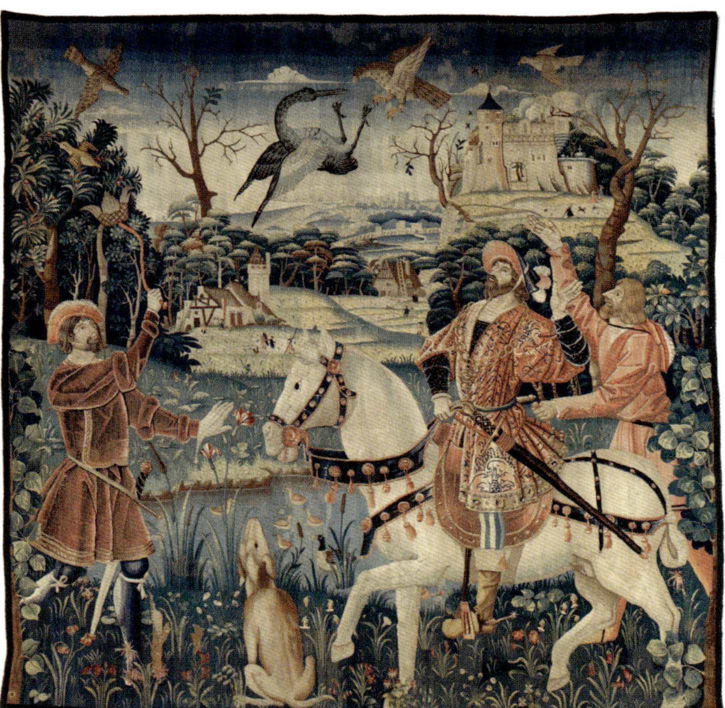

Fig. I
Fight Between a Falcon and a Heron, about 1525

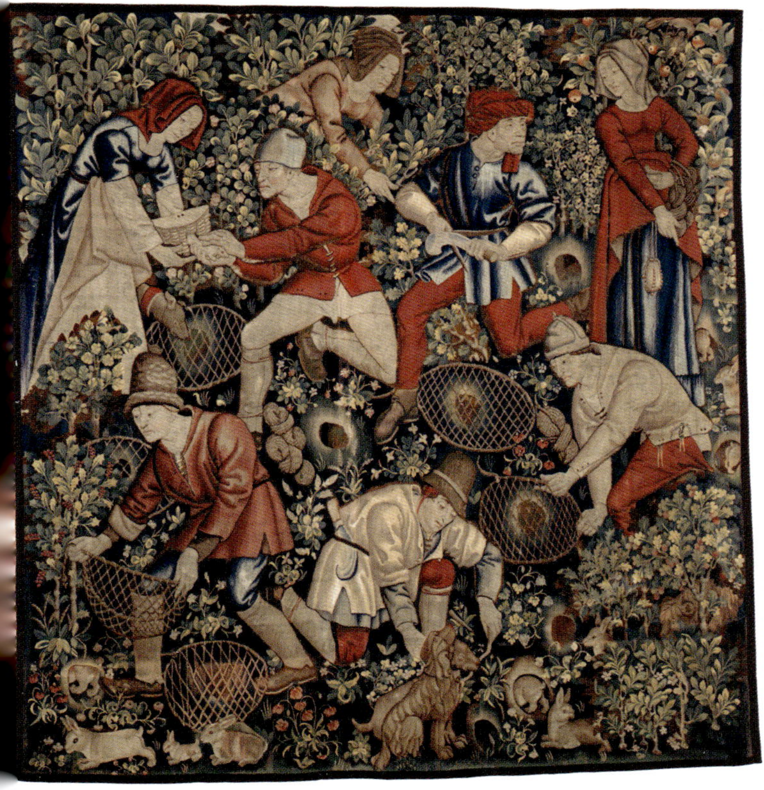

Fig. II
Peasants Preparing to Hunt Rabbits with Ferrets, about 1470–1490

I suspect that Burrell's relatively small expenditure on collecting until he was over 50 was a reflection of his main preoccupation with business. However, following the sale of most of the Burrell shipping fleet between 1913 and 1916, he clearly could devote much more time and money to focus on art. Additionally some of the great collectors such as Morgan and Frick died (1913 and 1919 respectively), and in the 1930s Hearst ran into serious financial problems during the Great Depression. This presented an opportunity for Burrell. Much of the medieval art he bought in the 1920s and 1930s went to furnish Hutton Castle, particularly the magnificent tapestries and stained glass that he acquired during this period. He was also able to buy spectacular pieces that would probably have been unavailable to him 20 years earlier. These include the wonderful tapestries of *Fight between a Falcon and a Heron* (46.60, *fig. I*) bought in 1936 and the tapestry of *Peasants Preparing to Hunt Rabbits with Ferrets* (46.56, *fig. II*) bought in 1939. The 'hunt' as a royal pursuit is something that resonates throughout the Collection, and Burrell himself, after settling into Hutton Castle, started playing the role of aristocratic landowner with frequent grouse shoots. In his collection this is reflected not only in the tapestries, but also in some of the paraphernalia of falconry, considered the most aristocratic of hunting pursuits throughout Europe and Asia and still practised actively today in the Middle East and Central Asia. Included in the exhibition are a falconry pouch (29.151.2), a falconry glove (29.151.1) and a swing lure (29.151.3), all made in Scotland or England between 1600 and 1609. Although these items are rather late for the chronology of the exhibition, they bring great value in illustrating a continuing aristocratic pastime and highlighting one of Burrell's abiding interests.

This is not to say that Burrell did not acquire any great objects before the purchase of Hutton Castle. In 1901 he had been the largest lender to the Glasgow International Exhibition, with over 200 loans. Burrell's generous support of the Exhibition (he was both sub-committee member and lender) is the first insight we have into the extent of his possessions. They show he owned a trove of medieval art, encompassing continental sculpture, English alabaster, tapestries, ivories, metalwork and stained glass. This initial core of objects established the character and parameters of Burrell's medieval collection that we know today. It remains most focused on objects from Germany, England, the Low Countries and France from the period 1350 to 1550, with a smattering of objects from Italy and Spain. At the same time, it is worth noting that he was also an active seller. In 1902 he put almost 40 paintings to auction, including works by Daumier and Manet. Periodically, Burrell would sell strategically in order to raise funds to buy other works that held greater appeal for him. Detailed Purchase Books kept by Burrell that survive from 1911 onwards confirm this behaviour, as they record the sale, exchange and trading-up of purchases, showing how Burrell tweaked the Collection over time.

Collectors are driven by many factors. Some collectors have a sensitivity to a particular period (e.g., medieval); some for a particular genre (tapestry, stained glass); some only want to have 'the best'; 'to complete the set'; or to acquire objects of great beauty. In my own case,

the first object I bought, 30 years ago, was an Italian Romanesque lion, and this acquisition started me on a learning journey that took me forwards in time to the Gothic and early Renaissance and backwards to the post-Roman and Byzantine periods. I started looking for cross-cultural connections: how did Byzantium influence western art? In plain terms it was through marriage – the Holy Roman Emperor Otto II married the Byzantine Princess Theophanu in 972AD which helped introduce Byzantine style to Northern Europe; through trade – the Venetians were trading with the Eastern Mediterranean and the Southern Italians were using Muslim craftsmen to make objects for export to Northern Europe; and through war – the Fourth Crusade sacked Constantinople (modern-day Istanbul) in 1204 and Crusaders brought back many marvels of

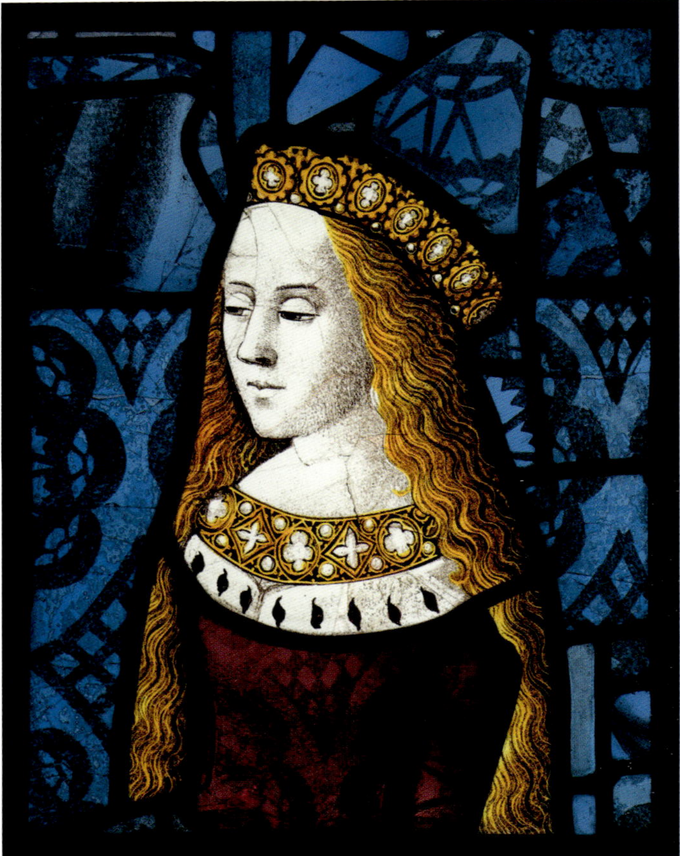

Fig. III
Princess Cecily, about 1482–1487

the ancient and Byzantine world which remain in St Mark's Cathedral in Venice to this day (not least of all the famous four Roman bronze horses known as the *Triumphal Quadriga*). It is these journeys of discovery that excite collectors. One such strand that emerges from Burrell's collecting is an attraction to objects that have strong historic provenance or even royal associations. The best examples might be the falconry pouch mentioned earlier, reputedly owned by King James VI and I (29.151.2) or the English stained glass panel depicting Princess Cecily, the daughter of Edward IV and Elizabeth Woodville (45.75, *fig. III*), which comes from the Royal window in Canterbury Cathedral.

If we review Burrell's medieval collections it is clear that his tapestries and stained glass are unparalleled in the UK, with the exception of the Victoria and Albert Museum, London. The range, quality and condition are wonderful and they are a great representation of the best that the artists in these fields could produce. Burrell bought over 200 tapestries, the majority dating from about 1450–1530, including outstanding works by known masters from every significant tapestry production centre during this period. Despite a reputation for being a 'bargain hunter', he also paid big prices for these works – one of the tapestries on display (*St Anne with Saints*, 46.16) cost £5,600 in 1928 and several others cost between £2,000 and £4,000. His sculpture collection has some wonderful highlights, such as the English medieval alabasters (which he loved for their British connections), especially the St John the Baptist tabernacles (1.33, 1.34, 1.35, *figs. IV*) and the large figure of the Trinity (1.2, *fig. V*). The St John tabernacles are fascinating as only five survive, three of which are in the Burrell Collection, with one of them (1.34, *fig. IV/A*) being the finest known. However, in general the quality of the sculpture, whilst strong, does not match the other areas in which he collected. One suspects it did not excite him in the same way (or maybe his 'eye' in this area was just not as good!), and he was clearly not prepared to invest as heavily in them. Most of the sculptures displayed here

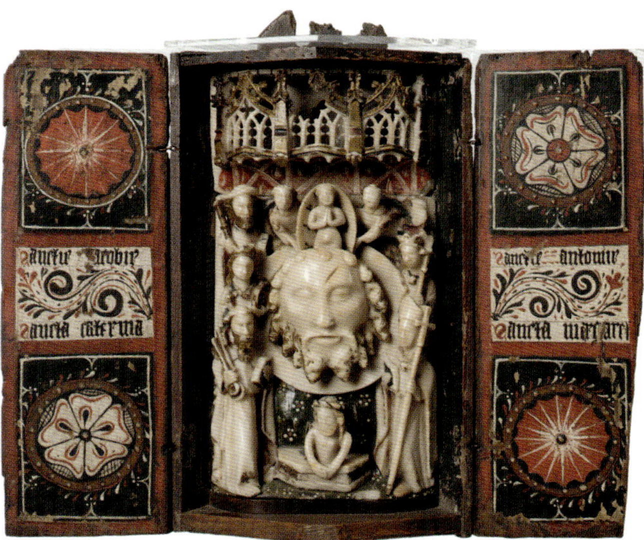

Fig. IV/A
Painted tabernacle with alabaster carving, late 1400s–early 1500s

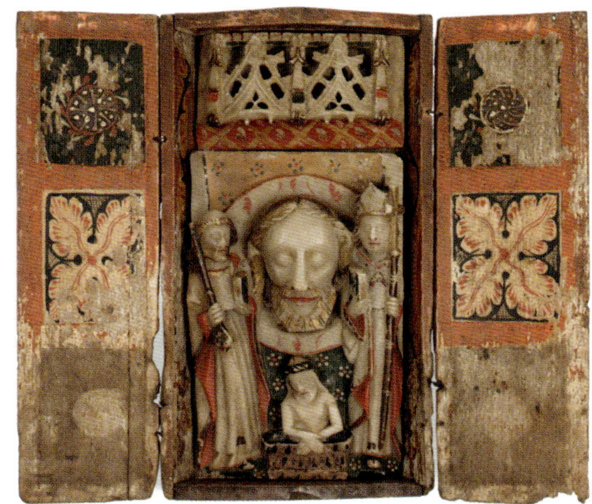

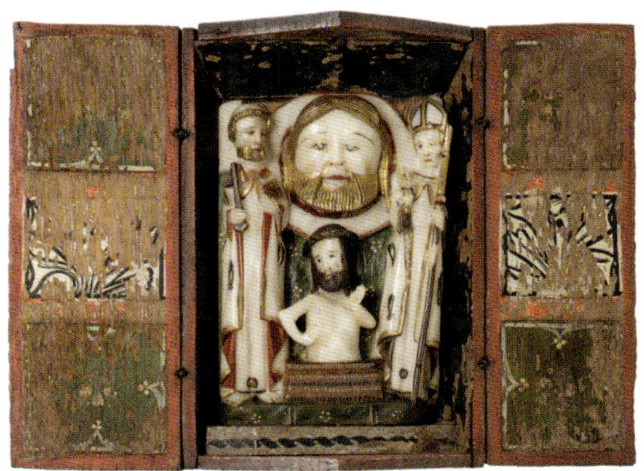

Fig. IV/B (right, above)
*Painted tabernacle with
alabaster carving,*
late 1400s–early 1500s

Fig. IV/C (right, bottom)
*Painted tabernacle with
alabaster carving,*
late 1400s–early 1500s

Fig. V
The Trinity: God the Father, Jesus Christ, and Souls of the Saved,
about 1400

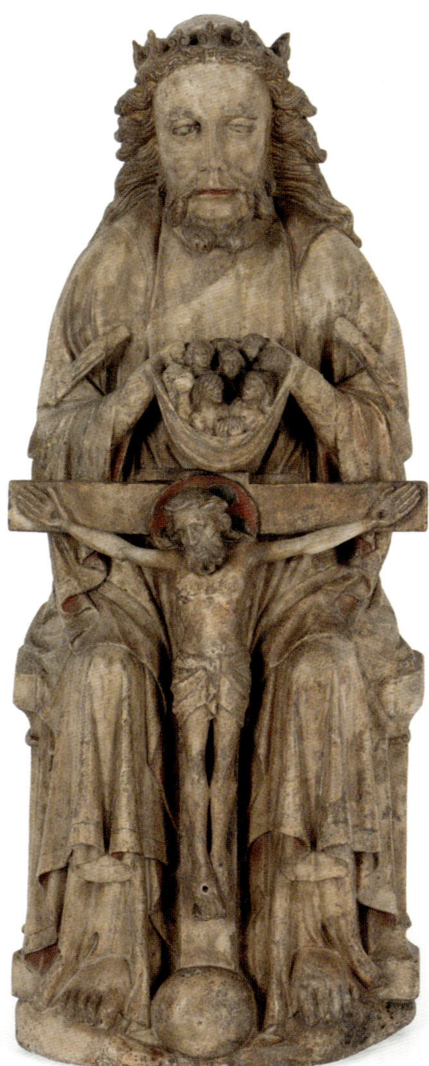

decorative art. Whilst he has a few spectacular small works – the *Temple Pyx* being the prime example (5-6.139, *fig. VI*), his Romanesque Limoges enamels are not generally in great condition, despite him buying them at a time when many better examples were available. Likewise, his small collection of Gothic ivories is good but not particularly special. The most expensive purchase was the *Temple Pyx*, bought in 1936 for £600, but for the ivories, enamels and bronzes he paid only between £100 and £300. Maybe he felt that he needed to 'flesh out the collection' rather than viewing these items as absolutely core to his collecting.

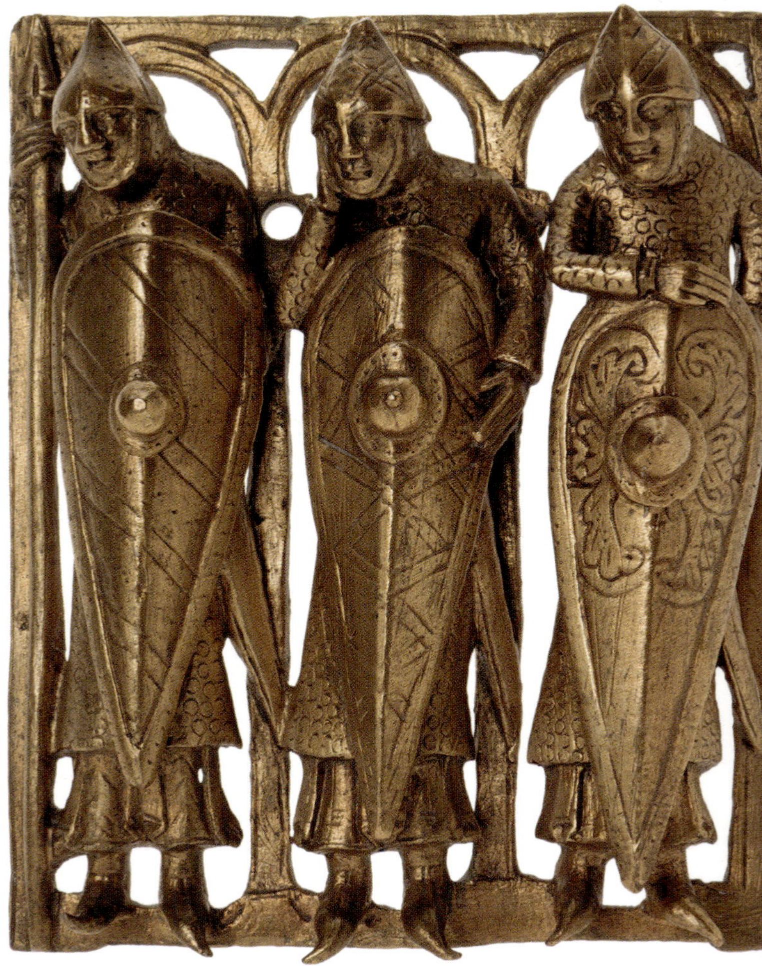

Fig. VI
Three sleeping soldiers at the Holy Sepulchre, called the Temple Pyx,
about 1140–1150

cost just a few hundred pounds. However, it is important to remember that he was also balancing other, non-medieval, collecting interests evidenced by the high volume of Chinese art that he acquired after 1911 and the individual works by significant Old Masters such as Bellini, Frans Hals and Rembrandt that came into the Collection in the 1930s and 40s. A similar system of priorities may have governed his purchase of medieval

Burrell also seemed to focus more intensively on different areas at different times. Most of the stained glass in the exhibition was bought in the late 1930s or the 1940s. Several smaller stained glass pieces were actually bought during World War II, in contrast to other areas in which he was collecting. A measure, however, of how determined his collecting of stained glass was up to 1930 is provided by Burrell's correspondence with his favoured stained glass dealer Wilfred Drake. In 1929, he writes to Drake declaring that his entire glass collection (at that point 222 panels) was now installed in the windows at Hutton Castle, including in the servants' quarters! Most of the 300 or so works of sculpture were acquired in the 1920s and 30s. The Purchase Books help to identify four distinct phases of collecting activity: the first from 1925 to 1933; the second from 1935 to 1939; the third in 1948 (when he acquired ten works in a single year); and the fourth between 1953 and 1957. The first period of intensity corresponds roughly with the completion of the renovations at Hutton Castle, which were finalized in 1932.

Tapestries were among his earliest interests. He lent 13 to the Glasgow International Exhibition in 1901 and photographs of his home at Great Western Terrace, Glasgow, taken the following year show that they lined the walls of landings, corridors and family rooms. They surmounted fireplaces and provided rich, colourful over-mantels. The accommodation of his tapestry collection at Hutton Castle determined much of the remodelling of the interior. In a letter of 1925 Burrell, who rarely recorded his opinion on the objects he collected, wrote 'of all of the Arts I think Tapestry and stained glass are two of the most attractive'. Indeed, until his acquisition of a self-portrait by Rembrandt in 1946, a late fifteenth-century tapestry of the *Distribution of the Vintage* had formed his single most expensive purchase. It is inconceivable in today's art market that a collector might spend more on a medieval tapestry than on a work by Degas or Manet!

He continued to acquire tapestries well into the 1930s at such volume that they could not all be accommodated at Hutton. He embarked on a generous scheme of loans to ensure that they could be appreciated by the general public, choosing to show them, for instance, in the medieval context of cathedrals across the UK. Burrell also lent regularly to exhibitions. He contributed tapestries, for example, to the 1936 Gothic Art show at the Burlington Art Club, London, as well as the already discussed alabaster Trinity (1.2, *fig. V*) and a very fine boxwood sculpture of the Virgin and Child (50.6, *fig. VII*). A willingness to share with the public brought home-grown collectors like Burrell a hero-like status in the British art world. Gothic art, wrote one, 'can only be acquired to-day by collectors with very long purses. In the last few years, the tendency has been for works of this period to cross the Atlantic, or be diverted, by an effort, into the safe harbour of one of the national museums. A few brave collectors continue to exercise

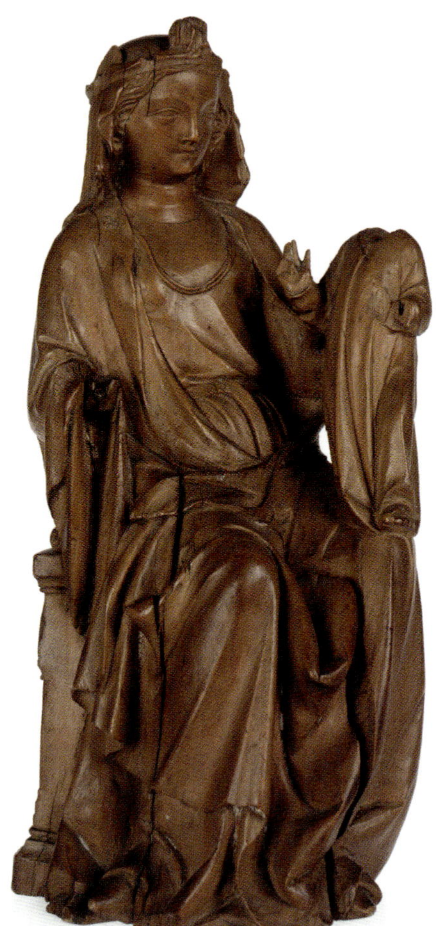

Fig. VII
Virgin Mary and Christ Child, about 1300

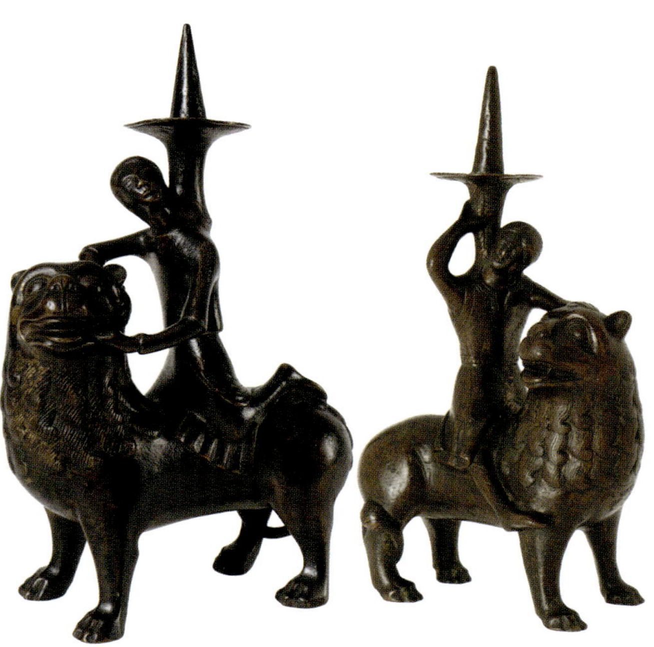
Fig. IX
Two candlesticks with Samson and the Lion, early 1200s

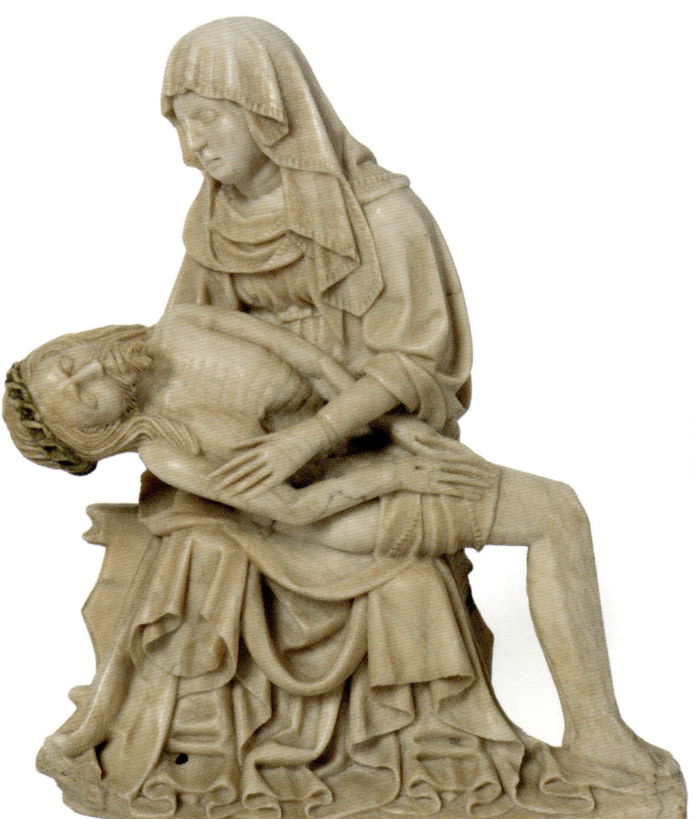
Fig. VIII
Virgin Mary with the dead body of Jesus Christ, 1440

the expensive rights of individualism, and some of
our ancient families and institutions loyally guard
the treasures which have been bequeathed to them'.
Burrell's generosity and philanthropy were confirmed
by the gift of his collection to the city of Glasgow in
1944 and by his voracious collecting to enhance the
gift, virtually up to his death in 1958. The wonderful
Pietà (Mary cradling the dead Christ, 1.25, *fig. VIII*) by
the workshop of the so-called Rimini Master, who was
active in the Netherlands in the 1430s, was bought by
him in 1955 when he was 94 years old! In the exhibition
there is another example for comparison of the same
subject from the same workshop, which is from my own
collection, previously owned by the celebrated collector
Robert von Hirsch.

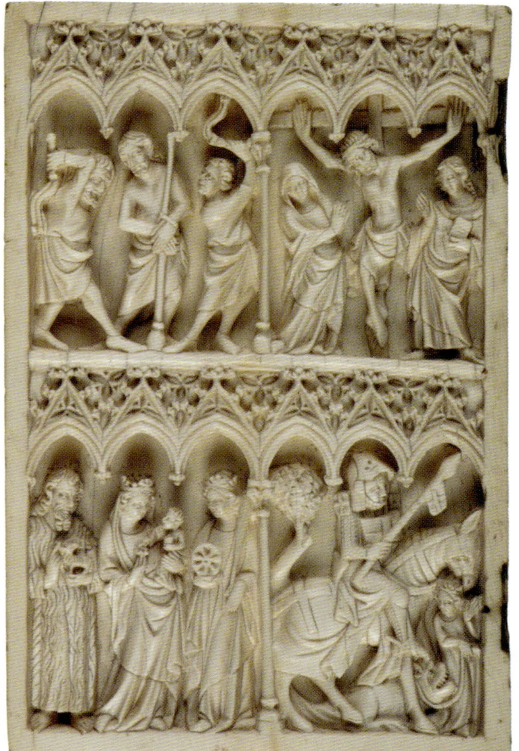
Fig. X
Left wing of a hinged folding diptych, about 1325–1375

Fig. XI (right)
Plaque for a book cover, late 1100s–early 1200s

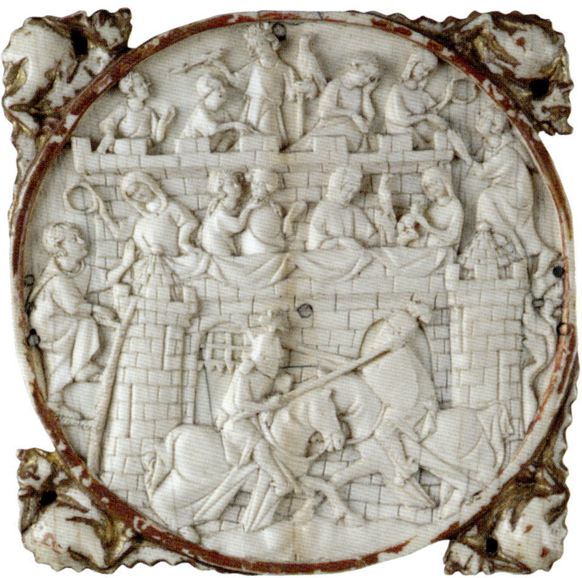

Fig. XII (above)
Mirror case showing the Castle of Love, about 1340

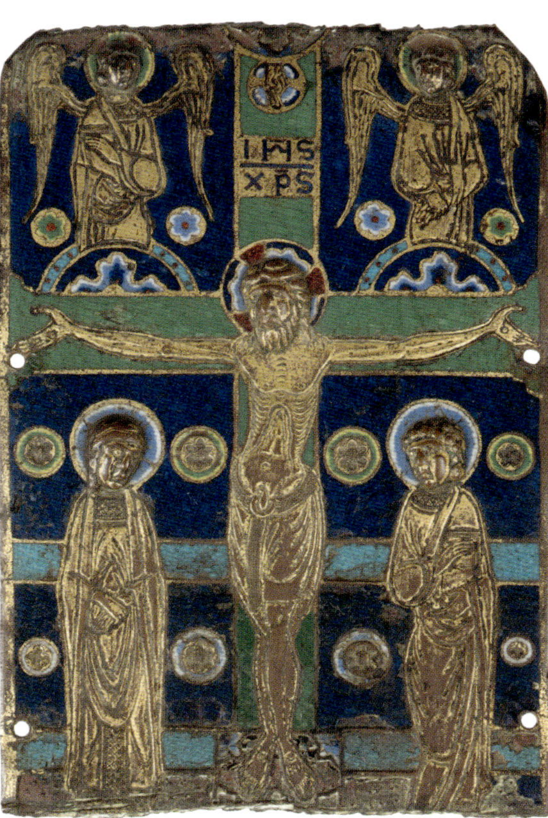

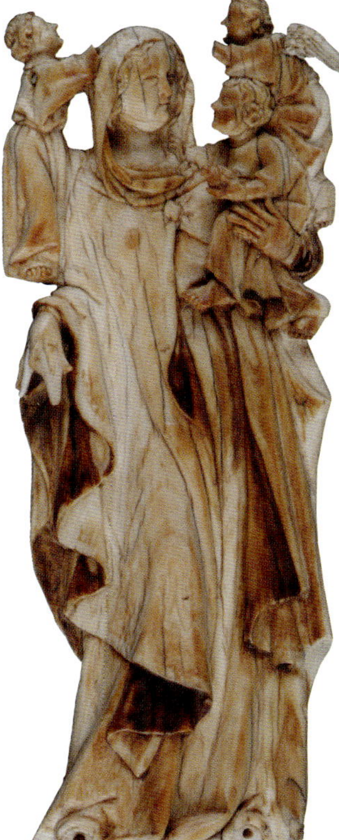

Fig. XIII (right)
Fragment of a decorated book binding, the Virgin Mary and Christ Child, late 1300s

Burrell clearly trusted certain dealers in specific areas and came to rely on their advice. But in the end, Burrell's medieval collection displays some of the idiosyncrasies of many great collectors as he refined or expanded his interests. Through this process he developed confidence in his own connoisseurship and secured a collection of worldwide renown that will bring enjoyment to visitors and scholars equally for generations to come. Had the Collection been dispersed at his death, the value of his very disciplined collecting would have been diminished. Now, however, as the Burrell enters a new period I am excited to contemplate its future as a centre of excellence for the display and study of tapestries and medieval stained glass. I hope too that this exhibition of the medieval highlights will give a glimpse of the magnificence of the Burrell Collection and a taste of what the newly renovated museum will offer.

Sir Paul Ruddock

MEDIEVAL TREASURES
from the Burrell Collection

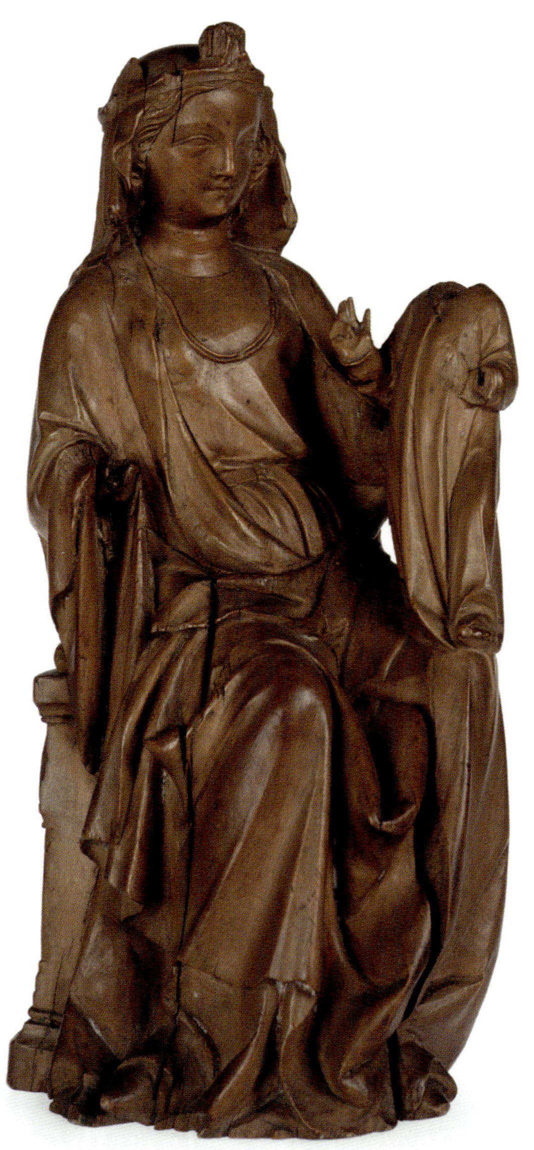

Wood

Virgin Mary and Christ Child, about 1300
Made in France, probably Paris, or in the
Upper Rhine Region, Germany
Boxwood, 328 x 163 x 133mm
50.6

Seated upon a barely visible throne, Mary's gaze
is directed towards the standing figure of Christ
balanced on her knee. His head and left hand are now
missing. So too, is his mother's right hand. This may
once have held a flower, perhaps a lily, or a fruit. The
crisp folds of her gown cascade away from the belt at
her waist, and fall weightily between her bent knees.
Her mantle, held in place by a crown, rests atop her
gently curling hair.

Boxwood, like ivory, was highly favoured by medieval
artists because of the high definition that could
be achieved when carved, and the glossy surface
that might be created by polishing. From the mid-
fourteenth century onwards it was frequently used
for making small objects such as spice boxes and
writing tablets, but relatively few larger scale works
such as this survive. This figure is one of several
boxwood carvings in the Collection, and one of two
gothic Virgin and Child statuettes.

Miniature cradle for a doll of the Infant Jesus, 1480–1500
Probably made in Brabant, the Southern Netherlands
Oak, paint, gilding, 253 x 190 x 115mm
50.239

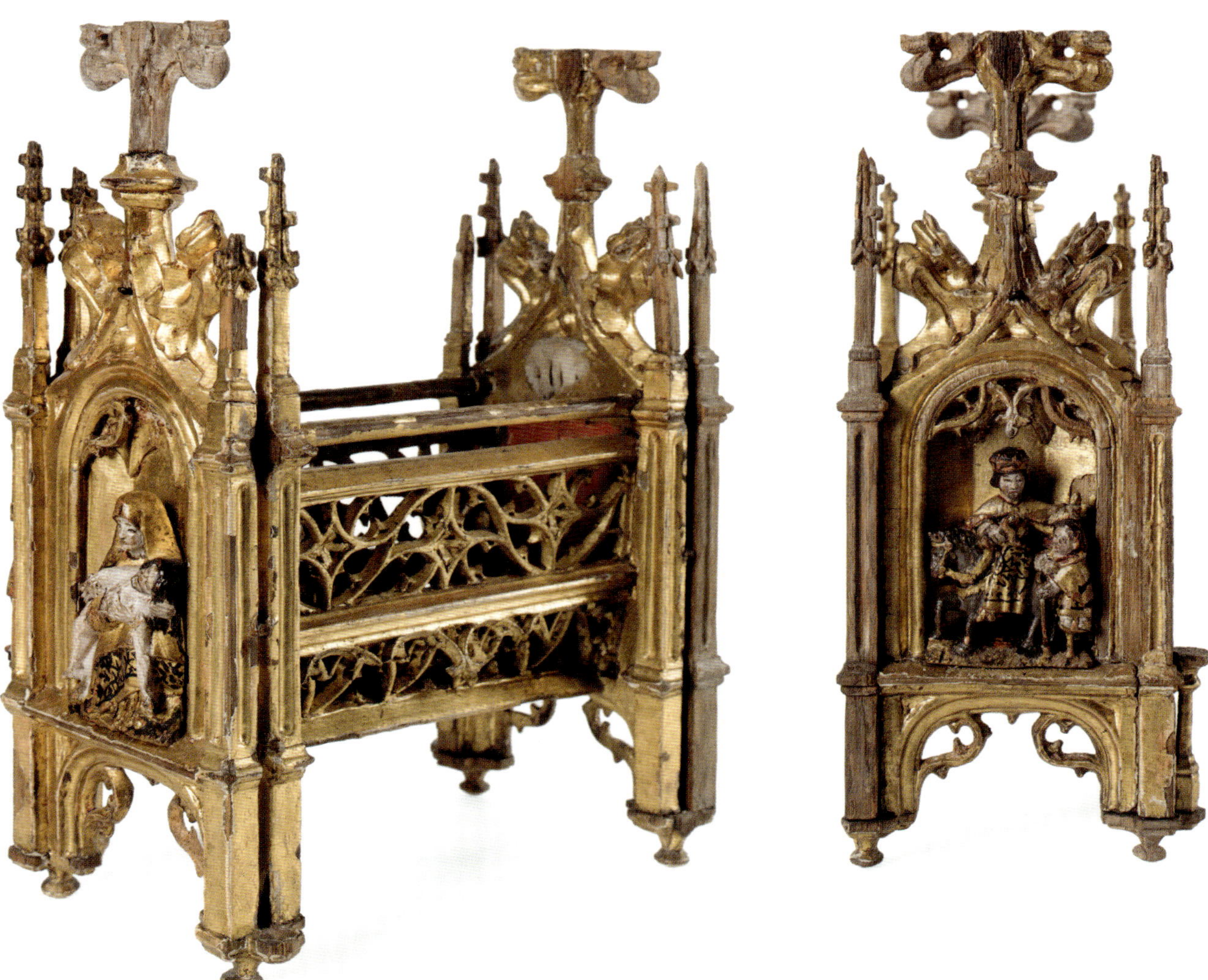

This little cradle may once have been part of a larger structure, suspended within a framework in which it could be moved to and fro. It is a rare survivor of a particular type of devotion which encouraged cloistered women to come closer to God by caring for a doll-like statue of the infant Jesus as if it were a real baby. This took the form of washing, swaddling and dressing the doll, laying him in the crib beneath embroidered sheets, rocking the cradle and mimicking lulling a real baby to sleep, for example through song. One end of the cradle is decorated with a *Pietà* (the dead Christ supported on his mother's lap), deliberately recalling the image of the Virgin and Child to poignant effect. The other end contains a representation of St Martin, the significance of which is not clear, although he may be the saint in whose name the convent was dedicated.

*St Catherine of
Alexandria,* 1490–1500
Probably made in the
Netherlands
Oak
1170 x 365 x 255mm

50.48

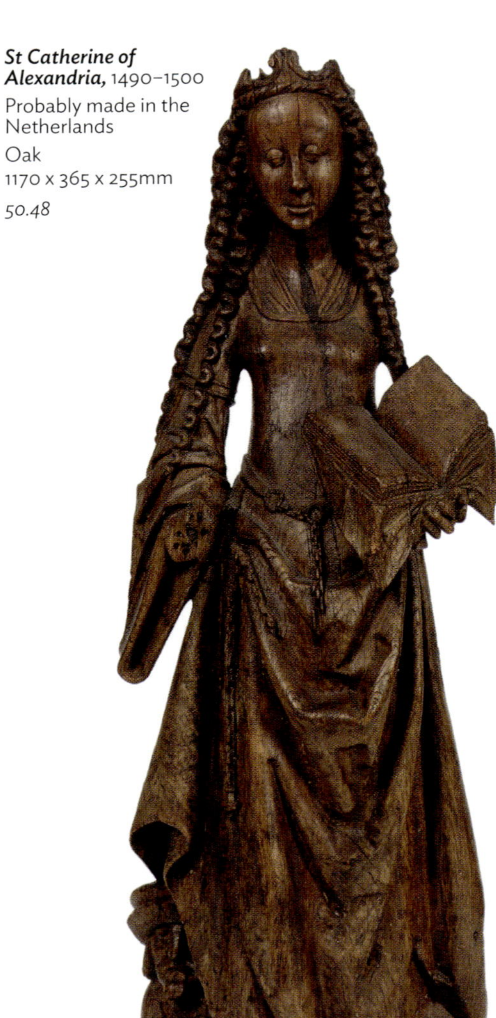

The Virgin Mary and Christ Child, about 1510
Made in Mechelen (Malines), Brabant,
the Southern Netherlands
Wood, polychromy, gilding, gemstones,
370 x 140 x 65mm

50.5

The Virgin Mary is shown standing with the Christ Child in her arm. He holds an apple whilst reaching for a bunch of grapes, a reference both to the fall of Man through the temptation of Eve and Man's redemption through Christ's sacrifice and the sacrament of the Eucharist. Known as *Poupées de Malines* (Dolls of Mechelen), these small, sweet figures were made in large numbers in the late fifteenth and early sixteenth centuries. The letter 'M' stamped into the tooled hem of her gown is the guarantee mark of the city's gilders.

Burrell's Purchase Book tells us that this figure of St Catherine was delivered directly from Paris to Dunbar. Though bought in the French capital, this sculpture is characteristic of Netherlandish work of around 1500. It shows St Catherine of Alexandria, a legendary princess who was murdered by the pagan emperor Maxentius, as part of his campaign against Christians. Maxentius sentenced Catherine to death by breaking her body on a spiked wheel, which shattered at her touch. He then ordered that she be beheaded. She is shown trampling Maxentius – a sign of Christianity's victory.

These flat-backed statuettes were used as single figures but also brought together with others in delicate and intricate altarpieces representing the garden of heaven. In this way the sculptures were embedded in a natural world constructed from parchment and cloth, and surrounded by written prayers, relics, trinkets, and votive offerings. The addition of a 'gem' stone to the headgear and bodice of this figure may be a sign that this too was once part of such a materially and texturally rich scene.

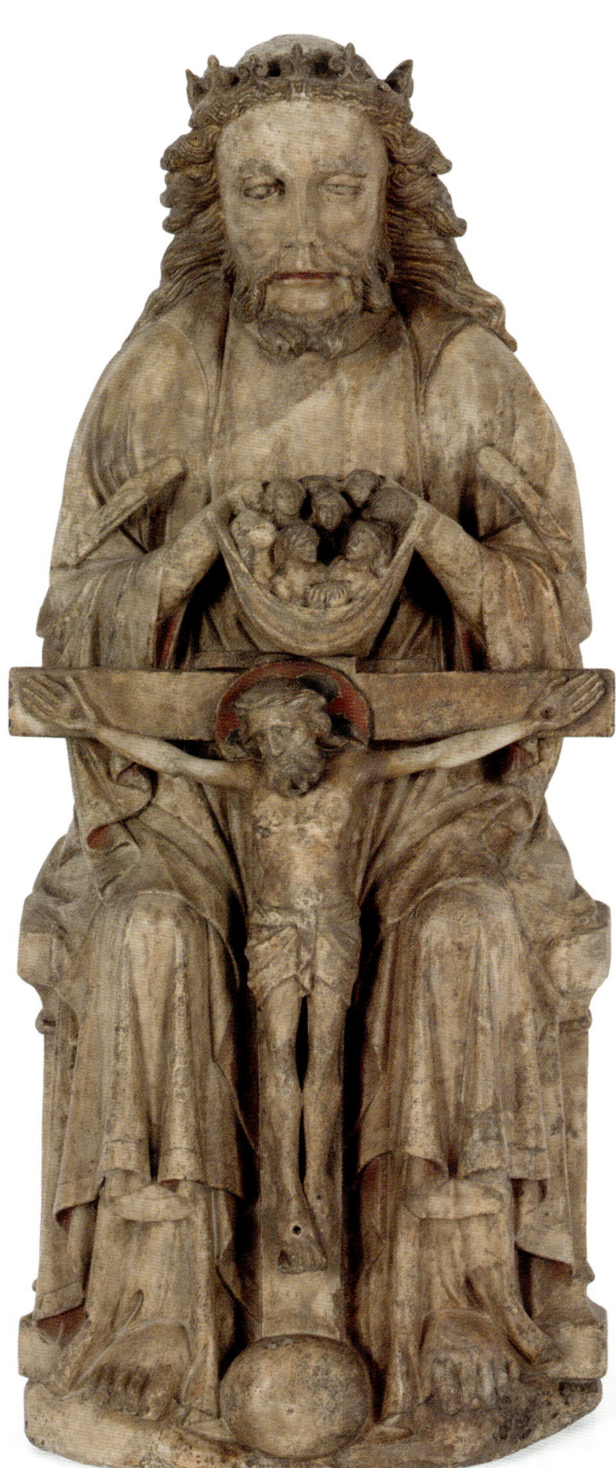

Alabaster

The Trinity: God the Father, Jesus Christ, and Souls of the Saved,
about 1400
Made in England
Alabaster, traces of colour, 900 x 330mm

1.2

English alabasters were very popular among both British and American collectors, so Burrell had to establish himself in the face of fierce competition. By keeping a careful eye on the market, he was able to gather an example of almost every type of alabaster produced from the mid fourteenth to the early sixteenth centuries, ranging from a large-scale, three-dimensional figure of the Virgin and Child to individual panels from altarpieces and small-scale figures of flanking saints. Burrell's alabasters reflect two main preoccupations: collecting multiple specimens of the same iconography or, conversely, collecting completely unparalleled examples. As a consequence of this collecting strategy, the Burrell Collection is home to a number of alabasters for which only very few related works are known to survive, not least among which is this important Trinity admired by art historian Nikolaus Pevsner as 'a piece of the highest emotional qualities'. Alabaster Trinities are relatively common, as they often formed the focus of altarpieces or chapels; 100 are known in total. Trinities featuring the souls of the blessed, seen here suspended in a napkin above the Crucifixion, are much rarer. Only 19 are known to survive.

Large painted tabernacle with alabaster carving, around 1480

Made in England

Painted oak, alabaster, traces of colour, 470 x 452 x 110mm (wings open)

1.34

Small painted tabernacle with alabaster carving, around 1480

Made in England

Painted oak, alabaster, traces of colour, 282 x 407 x 84mm (wings open)

1.33

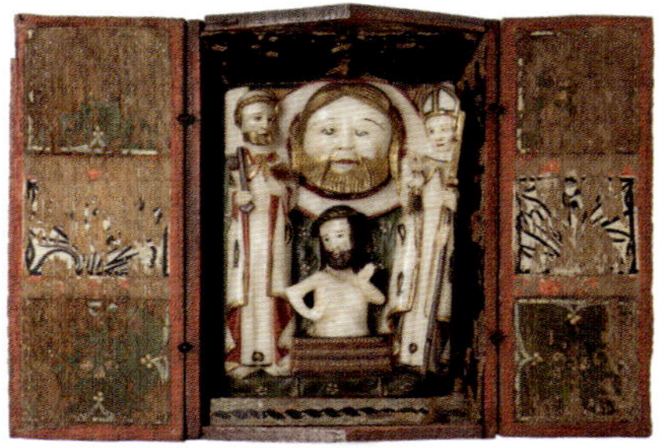

Medium painted tabernacle with alabaster, around 1480

Made in England

Painted oak, alabaster, traces of colour, 365 x 412 x 77mm (wings open)

1.35

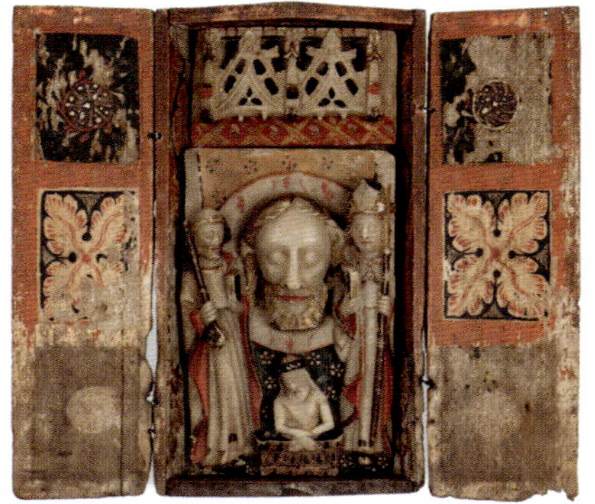

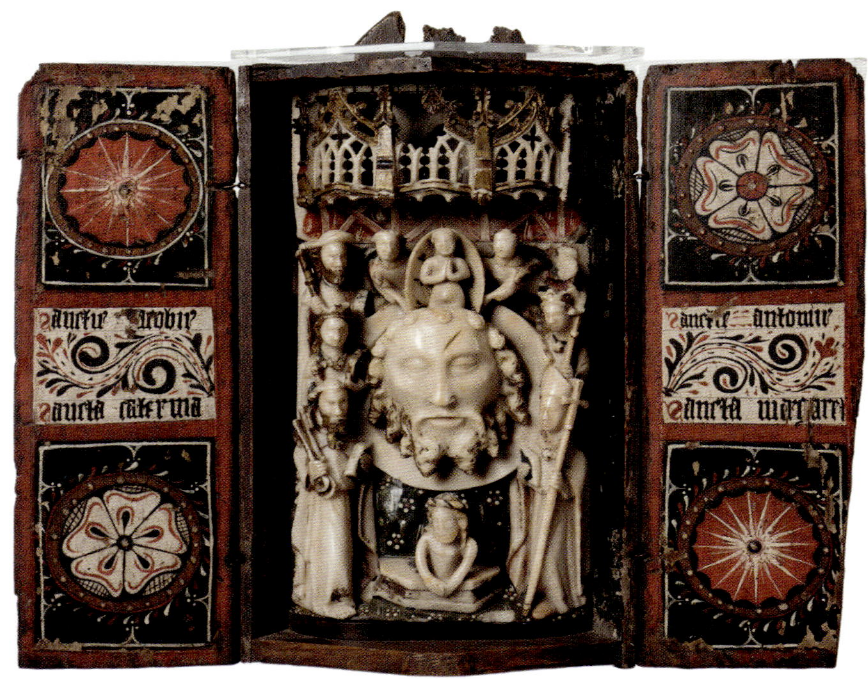

In the course of his collecting career, Burrell acquired three alabaster heads of St John the Baptist that still retain their original painted tabernacles. All three focus on the decapitated head of St John the Baptist, surrounded by figures of saints. Beneath, Christ rises from the tomb displaying the wounds of the Crucifixion. Two prominent figures flank the head of St John: St Peter on the left and a bishop on the right, most likely St Thomas Becket. In one of the three Burrell panels (1.34), four further saints are shown identified by their attributes and inscriptions on the wings as St James, St Margaret, St Anthony and St Catherine, and the head of St John is surmounted by two angels bearing his soul up to heaven.

In total only five such heads in tabernacles are known. The other two are in museums in Leicester and Carmarthen. The first of the three purchased by Burrell was probably bought in the 1890s as it came from the artist/dealer George Grosvenor Thomas who was active in Glasgow between about 1885 and 1899. Completely unknown to alabaster aficionados, the object was one of Burrell's first collecting coups and prompted him to seek out others. Over four decades Burrell quietly acquired a second and a third, each as unknown as the other. Of such differing qualities, this rare and unique assemblage allows us to appreciate how medieval makers tailored their responses to consumer spending power. They illustrate the trappings of medieval domestic devotion as opposed to the more monumental evidence for public worship provided by large-scale altarpieces in ecclesiastical settings.

Virgin Mary with the dead body of Jesus Christ, about 1440
School of 'The Rimini Master' (recently named as Gilles de Backere)
Made in the Southern Netherlands
Alabaster, traces of colour, 227 x 160 x 160mm
1.25

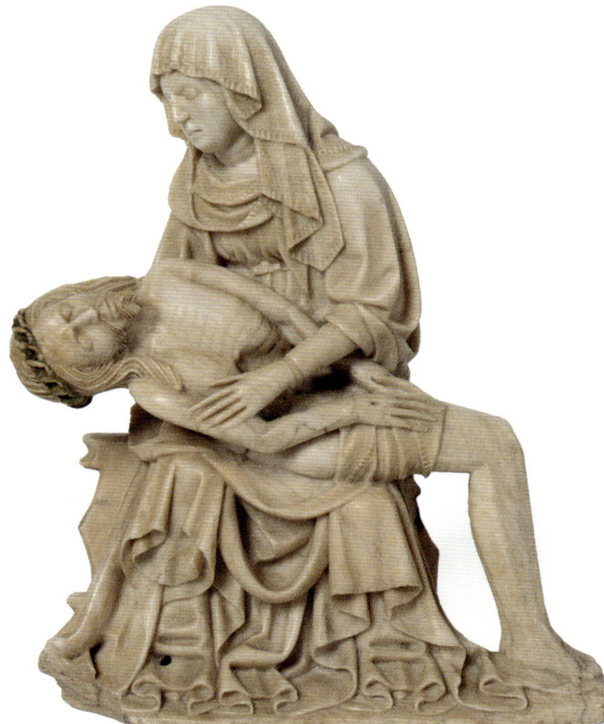

One of Burrell's most remarkable acquisitions, and also one of his very last, was an alabaster *Pietà*. Christ's broken body lies across the knees of the seated Virgin, his static lifeless frame met by her tender gaze. This scene, an artistic invention not derived from the Gospel narratives, gained great popularity across Europe as a means of conveying the emotional power of Christ's death in very human terms. The pose deliberately recalls the infant Christ nursed on his mother's lap.

Today, we know the work to be related to those by the Master of Rimini, a Southern Netherlandish craftsman named after the exquisite Crucifixion group from the church of Santa Maria delle Grazie in Rimini-Covignano, now at the Liebieghaus, Frankfurt am Main. It is most unlikely that Burrell was aware of this connection. Work on the Master of Rimini emerged mainly in the 1960s when Burrell was no longer alive to learn from it. Yet he is sure to have known that there was nothing else like it in any other UK museum. This acquisition for Glasgow would be the first Pietà of its type anywhere in the country (the Victoria and Albert Museum acquired its example in 1960).

Virgin Mary and Christ Child, about 1450–1475
Made in the Northern Netherlands
Alabaster, traces of colour, metal, 365 x 230 x 170mm
1.22

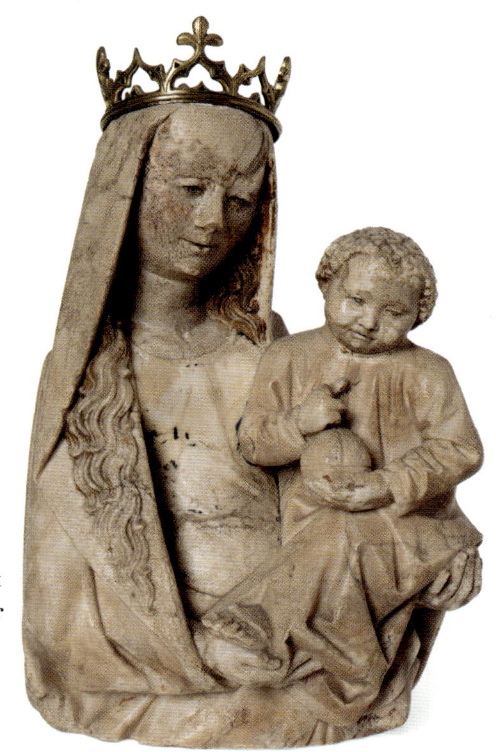

Burrell also acquired Continental sculptures made from grey veined alabaster, but never in the same number as he did English alabasters. This Virgin and Child is the most charming. Mary holds Jesus as if presenting him to the viewer. Her eyes are downcast, as are his, suggesting that the sculpture was intended to be positioned on high. Jesus holds an orb, signalling his role as saviour of the world.

Despite the strong character of this piece, it has proven impossible to link it with a particular artist. It is likely that the work was made by a sculptor associated with the Burgundian court, perhaps with a knowledge of the work of the Spanish artist Jean de la Huerta, for the Christ Child shows a clear relationship with the Christ of his Virgin and Child (known as the Vierge des Capucins) in the Church of Saint-Hilaire, Pesmes.

Stone

Virgin Mary and the Christ Child,
about 1330–1340
Made in Île de France, France
Limestone, painted glass,
1285 x 420 x 260mm
44.2

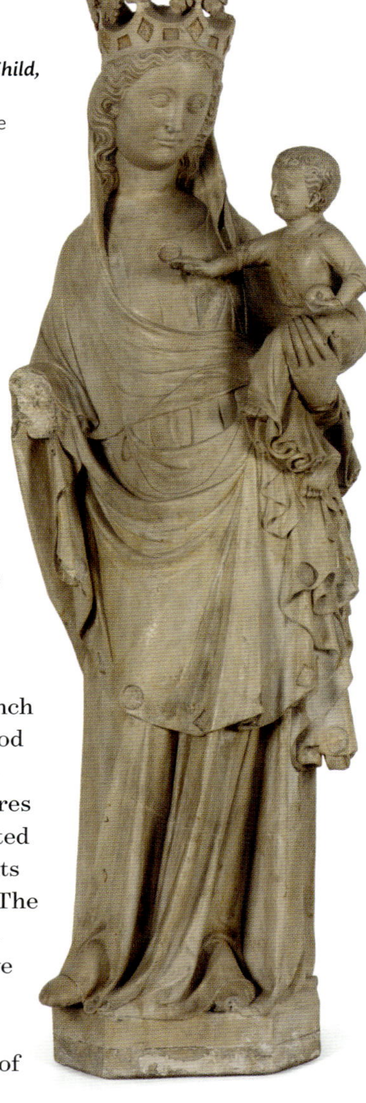

With her refined regal features and high foliated crown, this limestone Virgin and Child probably originated somewhere in Paris or the Île-de-France. It may have been removed from a church during the French Revolution or the period of state secularization that ensued. Such figures were once subtly painted with the finest pigments and gilded highlights. The Christ Child, balanced on her arm, would have been enlivened with ruddy cheeks and a piercing gaze. Echoes of this richness remain. Pieces of glass have been set into the hem of the Virgin's robe where they were intended to simulate precious gems and cameos. Her crown too was originally enhanced in this way. It is extremely rare for these fragile vestiges of medieval ornament to survive in any works of stone.

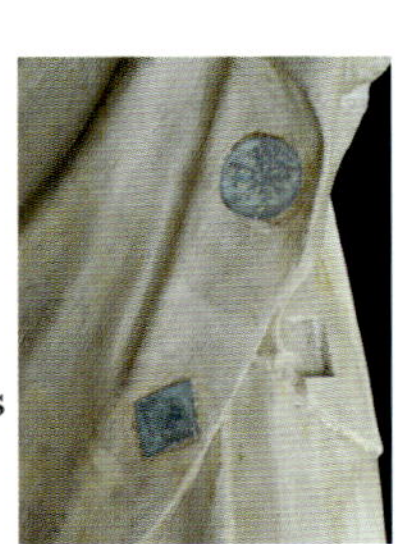

St Martha and the Tarasque, late 1400s–early 1500s
Probably made in Provence, Southern France
Limestone, traces of colour, 1630 x 500 x 410mm
44.20

Burrell's occupancy of Hutton Castle from about 1927 may have influenced his purchase of larger-scale works such as this figure of St Martha. Her story is related in *The Golden Legend*, a popular book of saints' lives that was as widely known as the Bible in the Middle Ages. It describes how Martha, the sister of Lazarus who was raised from the dead by Jesus, travelled to France where she encountered a fearsome dragon (a tarasque) that inhabited the marshland between Arles and Avignon. She tamed the monster through prayer and song and subsequently became the focus of a popular cult at Tarascon, a town named after the mythical beast. In 1949, a London critic saw St Martha in an exhibition in Glasgow and questioned the authenticity of the work. Burrell contacted its seller who wrote back citing the fact that he had been permitted to exhibit the work at the *Exposition Internationale des Arts et Techniques dans la Vie Moderne* (May–November 1937) as evidence that it had passed an expert vetting committee.

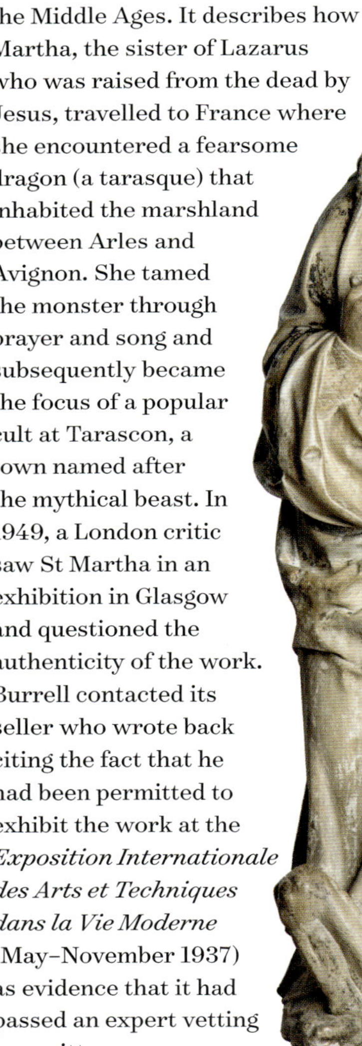

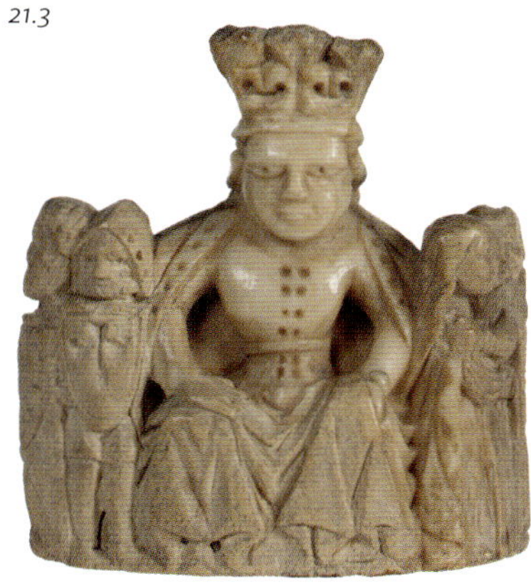

Ivory

All of the ivories in the Burrell Collection were made before the 1989 ban on the international trade of elephant ivory.

Chess piece, an enthroned queen, late 1300s/early 1400s
Made in Scandinavia or Germany
Walrus ivory, 75 x 71 x 25mm
21.3

A stately queen gazes ahead of her, seated between standing, but still much smaller, attendants. Her high crown, tight-fitting bodice, throne and plaited tresses have been rendered with attention to detail. The queen piece, with its ability to make complex moves, became the most powerful piece on the chessboard from the fifteenth century onwards.

Burrell was an avid chess player and was undoubtedly attracted to this miniature sculpture as much for its function as its form. When combined with the rarity of medieval figural chess pieces this must have seemed a truly irresistible acquisition. He noted their scarcity in his Purchase Book, highlighting the lack of comparative literature available to him.

Panel from a casket, 1300s
Made in England or France
Elephant ivory, 173 x 159 x 5mm
21.16

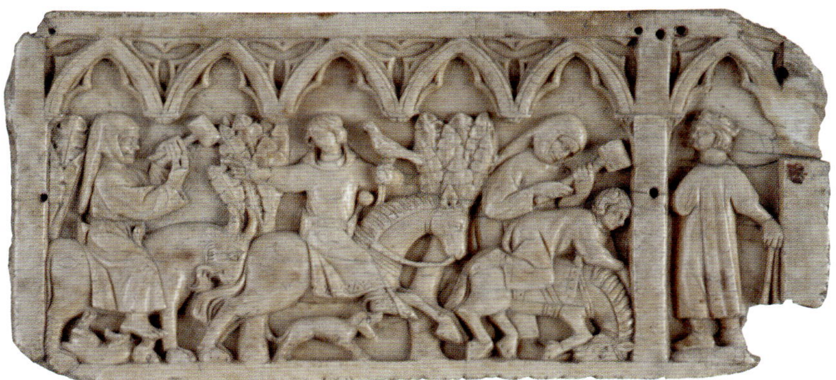

This panel, possibly from the front of a casket, tells a baffling story. A hooded man riding a goat and wielding a club pursues a youth mounted on horseback equipped for the hunt. In another scene, the man bludgeons the youth and the horse. The narrative is most likely drawn from a popular tale of courtly romance, but it has yet to be identified.

Mirror case showing the Castle of Love, about 1340
Made in Paris, France
Elephant ivory, 121 x 121 x 15mm
21.10

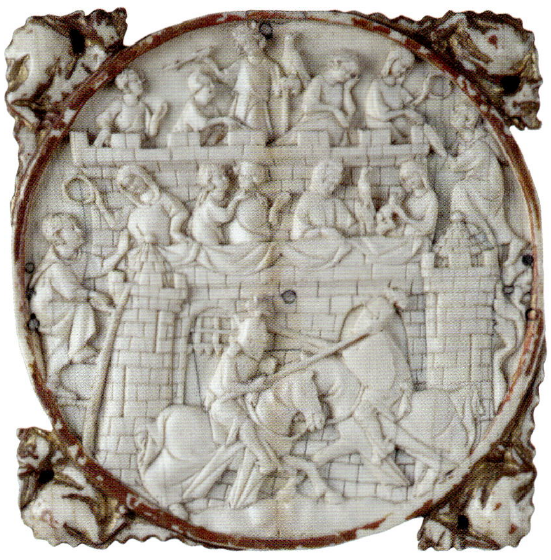

Despite high competition and high prices, Burrell was able to acquire a number of good quality ivories. Among the most splendid is this case for a polished metal mirror (now lost). It shows knights jousting before a castle where ardent suitors scale the ramparts. Ladies hold garlands with which to crown them on arrival. Surmounting it all, the God of Love stands aloft, ready with his heart-piercing arrow.

Left wing of a hinged diptych, about 1325–1375
Made in France
Elephant ivory, 169 x 110 x 12mm
21.9

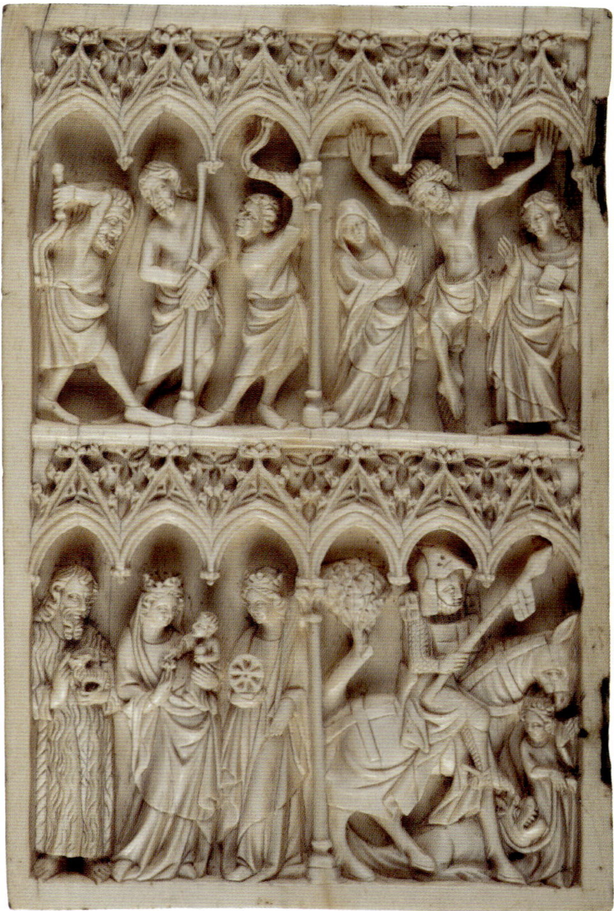

Fragment of a decorated book binding, the Virgin and Child with Angels,
late 1300s
Probably made in the Middle Rhine Region, Germany
Elephant ivory, 185 x 77 x 20mm
21.13

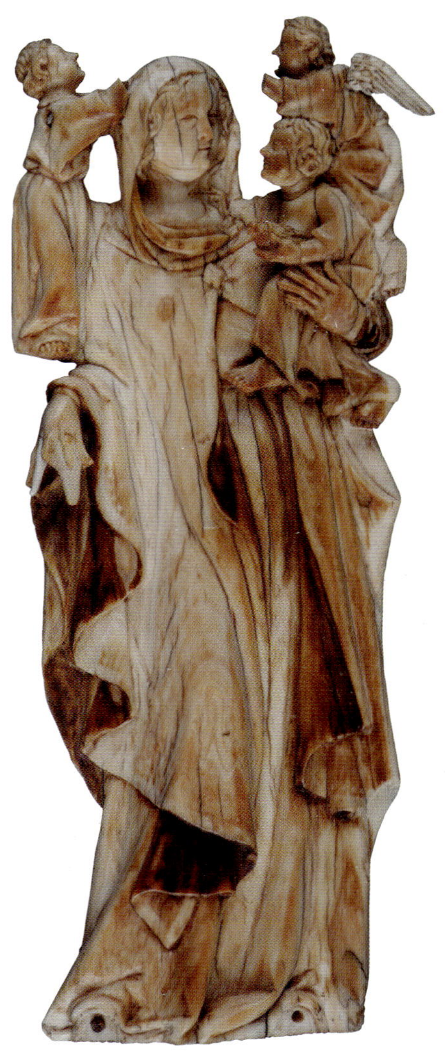

This panel was once part of a hinged altarpiece known as a diptych. The top half shows the flagellation of Christ while the bottom half depicts the Virgin and Child with St John the Baptist, St Catherine and St George. After Burrell's death, the corresponding right panel was identified in the British Museum. There since 1885, it is accompanied by a note stating that it was found under a 'hog trough' near Mansfield in Nottinghamshire, and in the seventeenth and first half of the eighteenth century was owned by the Fisher family of Grantham. No mention is made of the Burrell piece. The original object had clearly already been long dismantled when found.

Burrell acquired this figure of a Virgin and Child as a sculpture, but the item is of such slender dimensions that it must have been applied to another object, perhaps a book cover or a small altarpiece. The stylistic features are unusual, but certain details recall German works from the period around 1350 to 1375 and may place this figure as Middle Rhenish.

Metalwork

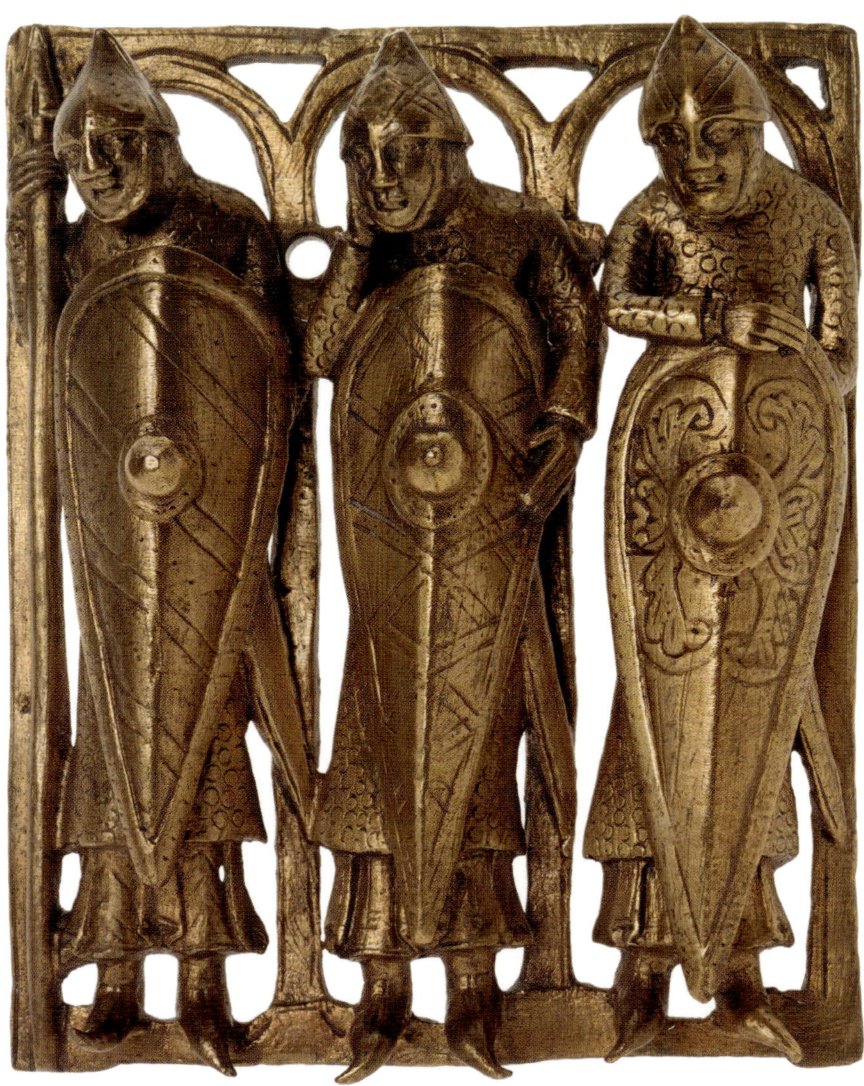

***Three sleeping soldiers at the Holy Sepulchre,
called the Temple Pyx,*** about 1140–1150

England or Meuse Valley (present-day
Belgium and Germany)

Gilt copper alloy, 92 x 73 x 20mm

5-6.139

An undisputed masterpiece of Romanesque metalwork,
this openwork mount representing three sleeping soldiers
is uncharacteristic of Burrell's interest in medieval
art due to its early date. Its rarity and provenance (as
understood at the time) clearly exerted great appeal
for Burrell, but a particularly persuasive factor in his
purchase of it seems to have been his desire to protect
it from leaving the UK for a collection in the United
States. The item takes its name from its reported place
of discovery. A note in *The Gentleman's Magazine* of
1833 refers to it being found in the Temple Church,
London during 'recent' repairs. In 1941, however, further
evidence was published to cast doubt on this information.
A drawing was discovered showing it with five other
mounts. An explanatory note describes them as
'… found in the cabinet of the late Revd. Mr Betham
Fellow of Eton College, and apprehended to be taken from
a Tomb-Stone, of the age of William the Conqueror'. The
associated pieces have not yet come to light. Questions
still surround its function. Long considered to be a
fragment from a pyx (a container for the consecrated
host), it is more likely that it formed part of book cover,
shrine or reliquary representing the three soldiers who
slept at the tomb while Christ was resurrected.

Plaque for a book cover showing the Crucifixion of Jesus Christ, the Virgin Mary and St John the Evangelist, late 1100s–early 1200s
Made in Limoges, France
Copper, enamel, gold, 169 x 112 x 5mm
26.1

The French city of Limoges became famous for the large amounts of enamelled metalwork it produced from the twelfth to the fourteenth century. Among the many items that were made there were plaques such as this, designed to embellish sacred texts and other books. Those showing the Crucifixion were often combined with plaques showing Christ in Majesty surrounded by the symbols of the four Evangelists.

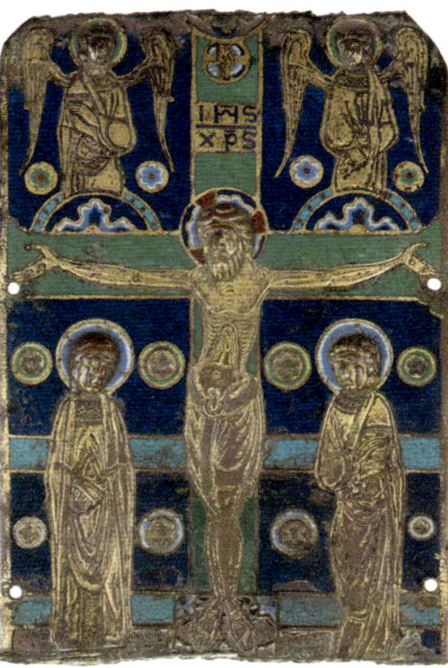

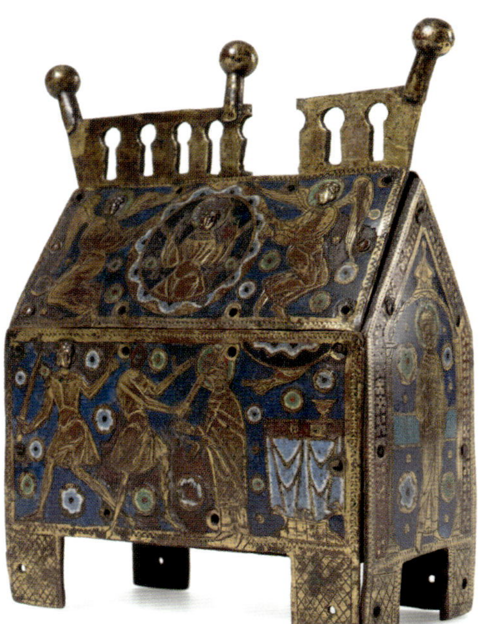

Reliquary casket (called a châsse) showing the murder of Thomas Becket, Archbishop of Canterbury, about 1200–1210
Made in Limoges, France
Copper, enamel, gold, wood core, 171 x 121 x 70mm
26.6

This reliquary casket (left) shows the murder of St Thomas Becket, Archbishop of Canterbury, in December 1170. The cathedral site of his sacrilegious death immediately became a place of spontaneous popular pilgrimage. Becket was canonized in 1173 and his relics were carefully circulated in precious reliquaries, such as this, to promote devotion. The casket came with collecting pedigree: its owners had all been distinguished figures. Burrell acquired it from Leopold Hirsch but it had also been owned by Walter Sneyd and Horace Walpole. Walpole's neo-gothic home, Strawberry Hill in London, gave birth to the resurgence of interest in the medieval gothic style that so dominated Burrell's home at Hutton Castle. Excitingly, the reliquary could even be traced back further through Thomas Barrett of Lee Priory, near Canterbury, to John Batteley, Archdeacon of Canterbury Cathedral where Becket's shrine had attracted countless pilgrims before its destruction by Henry VIII.

Two candlesticks with Samson and the Lion, early 1200s
Made in the Meuse Valley
Copper alloy, 305 x 187 x 85mm and 296 x 200 x 97mm
5-6.25 and 5-6.26

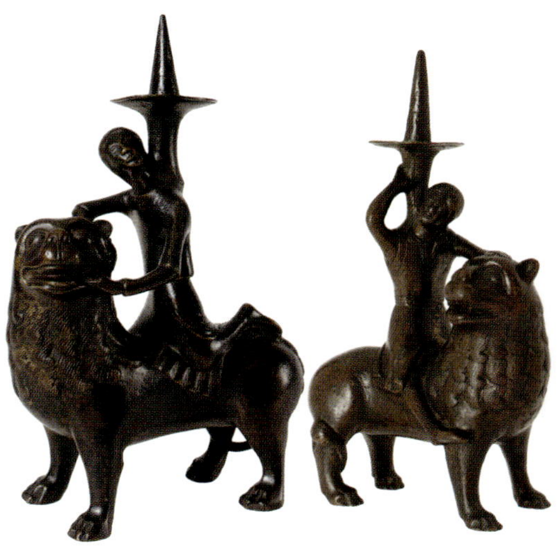

Although these two pricket candlesticks represent the famous episode of Samson and the Lion taken from the biblical book of Judges (14:5–7), they may have been used in either a sacred or a secular setting. Samson was a popular figure in medieval secular aristocratic art because of his strength, valour and virtue.

These two candlesticks have been treated as a pair since at least 1935, when they were both in the hands of the Hungarian dealer and collector Alexander von Frey. He had acquired one (5-6.26) from the collection of Sigismund Bardac and the other (5-6.25) had previously been in Weimar. A seminal publication of the same year suggested that they were so similar that they must have been made in the same workshop and lauded them as 'masterpieces of the genre'.

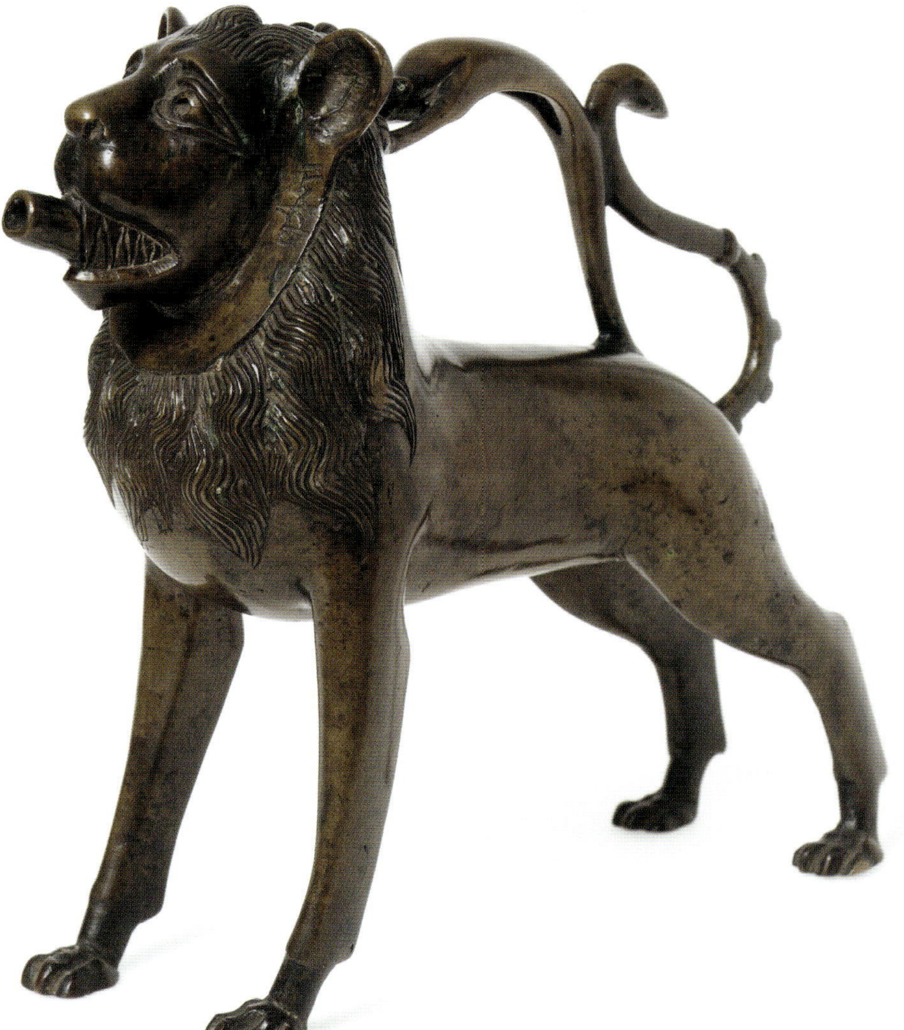

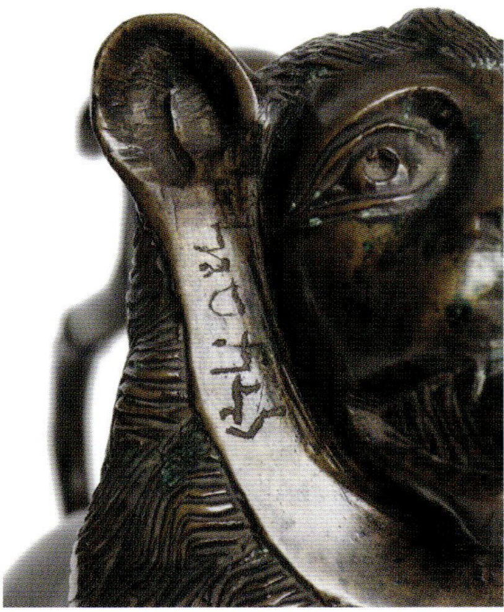

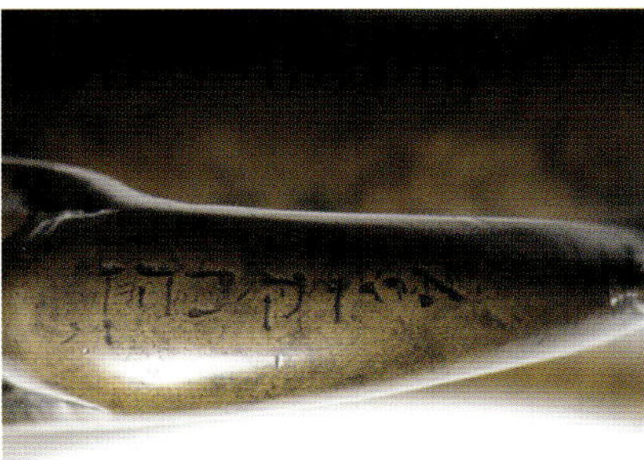

*Aquamanile inscribed 'Isaac Cohen',
'Lea Segal' and 'Wolfe' in Hebrew,* around 1300
Made in Lower Saxony, northern Germany
Copper alloy, 286 x 110 x 307mm
5·6.9

Aquamaniles were used in hand washing, an essential component of medieval religious ritual and secular banqueting. Their usually anthropomorphic forms proved especially popular with collectors in the nineteenth and early twentieth centuries, and they were frequently reproduced as well as faked. Burrell fell into the trap of unknowingly acquiring at least one copy. Yet such errors were balanced by spectacular acquisitions such as this wonderful aquamanile in the form of a lion that carries inscriptions in Hebrew. As one of only four known to exist, it is rare evidence of medieval Jewish material culture. In synagogues, as in Christian contexts, aquamaniles were likely used for the ceremonial hand washing of the celebrant, but at least one of the surviving examples is likely to have been used at home to hold the wine used at Kiddush.

Drinking horn inscribed 'Co(n)r(a)d Durekop',
before 1536
Possibly made in Riga, Latvia, reworked in
Vienna around 1826
Gilt-silver, possibly cow horn,
267 x 290 x 120mm

43.12

Horns like these were used at
court, by the nobility, clergy and
guildsmen. Their existence is
captured in many contemporary
paintings, particularly depictions of
the Three Magi, where a precious
golden horn is one of their gifts.
Referring to this, the smaller of
Burrell's curving horns is inscribed
with the names by which the Magi
are often known – Caspar, Melchior
and Balthazar. Its tip is capped
by an acorn-like curving finial,
pointing to a Scandinavian origin,
perhaps Denmark. The other, with
its later wild men feet, has Baltic
connections. It bears an inscription
linking the work to Conrad Durkop.
The Durkop family were important
burgers of the Hanseatic Riga,
and there were many Conrads
among them, nearly all politically
significant figures. The most famous
among them played a major role in
the introduction of the Reformation
to the city in the first half of the
sixteenth century.

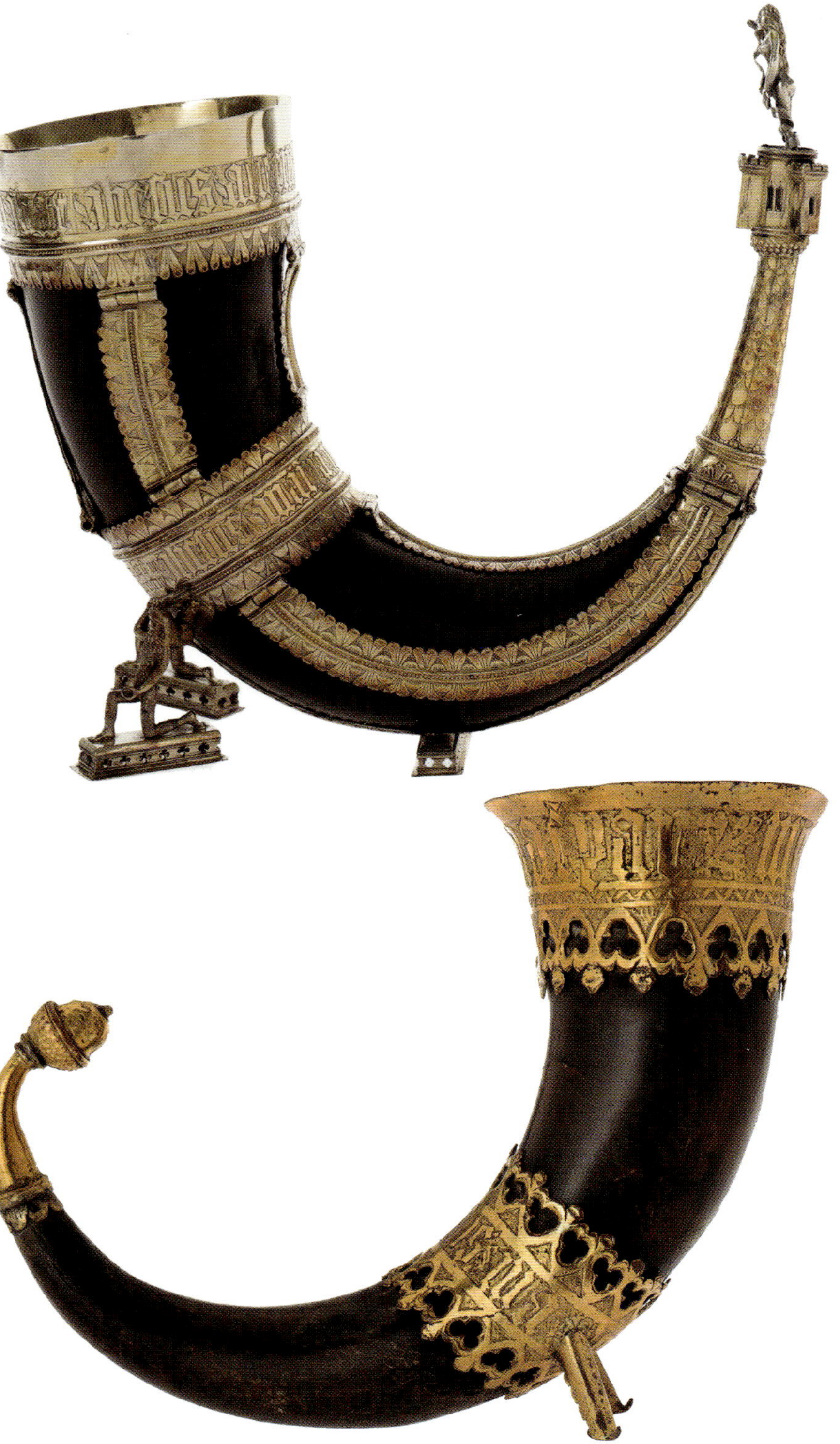

Drinking horn inscribed
'Caspar, Melchior and Balthazar', 1400s
Possibly made in Denmark
Gilt-silver, possibly cow horn,
165 x 212 x 86mm

21.21

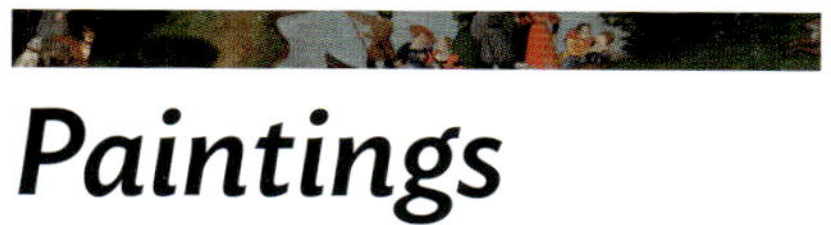

Paintings

The Stag Hunt, 1529
Studio of Lucas Cranach the Elder (1472–1553)
Oil on panel
1045 x 1441 x 150mm framed
36.73

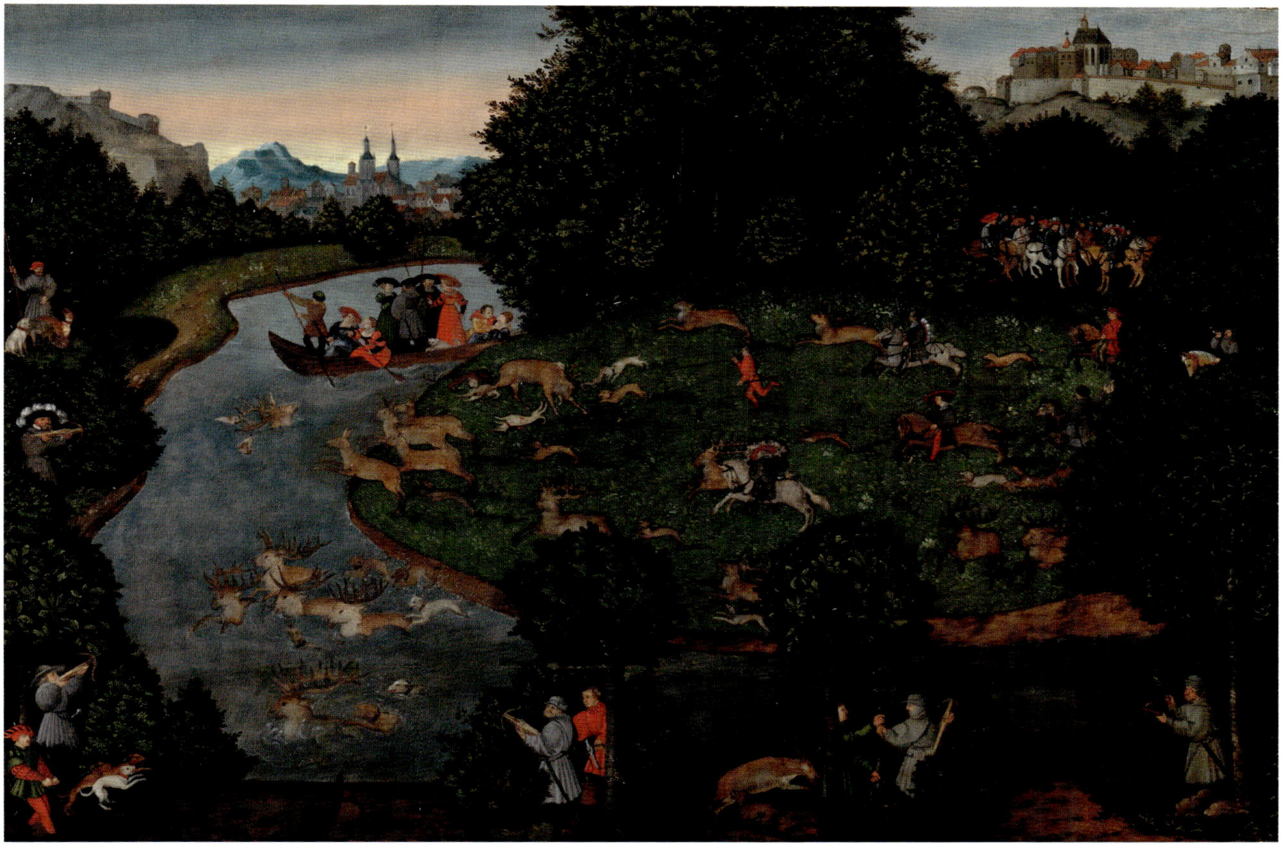

Burrell acquired three paintings by Cranach. One, *Cupid and Venus: the Honey Thief* (1545) was photographed in the Burrells' first marital home at 8 Great Western Terrace, Glasgow, where they lived from 1901. It is not known when Burrell acquired Cranach's beautifully detailed depiction of *The Stag Hunt,* but it too could have been in his possession by this date. He had visited Vienna several times and was probably familiar with the version of the same painting at the Kunsthistorisches Museum. He may also have known the third example in Copenhagen. The royal provenances of these two related paintings suggest that an equally princely audience had once enjoyed the painting that Burrell now owned.

The Virgin Annunciate, about 1465–1470
Attributed to the Master of the Prado
Adoration of the Magi (active about
1450–1475)
Oil on panel, 685 x 465 x 50mm framed
35.353

The Flight into Egypt, about 1465–1470
Attributed to the Master of the Prado *Adoration of the Magi*
(active about 1450–1475)
Oil on panel, 685 x 640 x 60mm framed
35.532

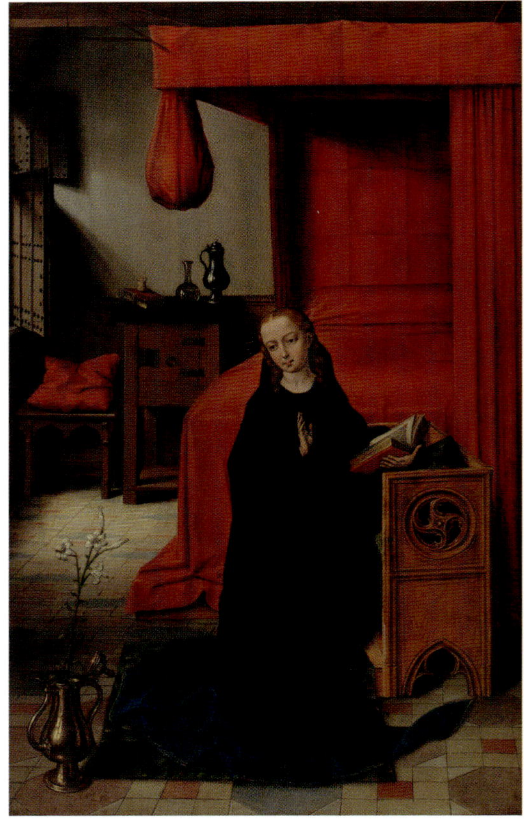

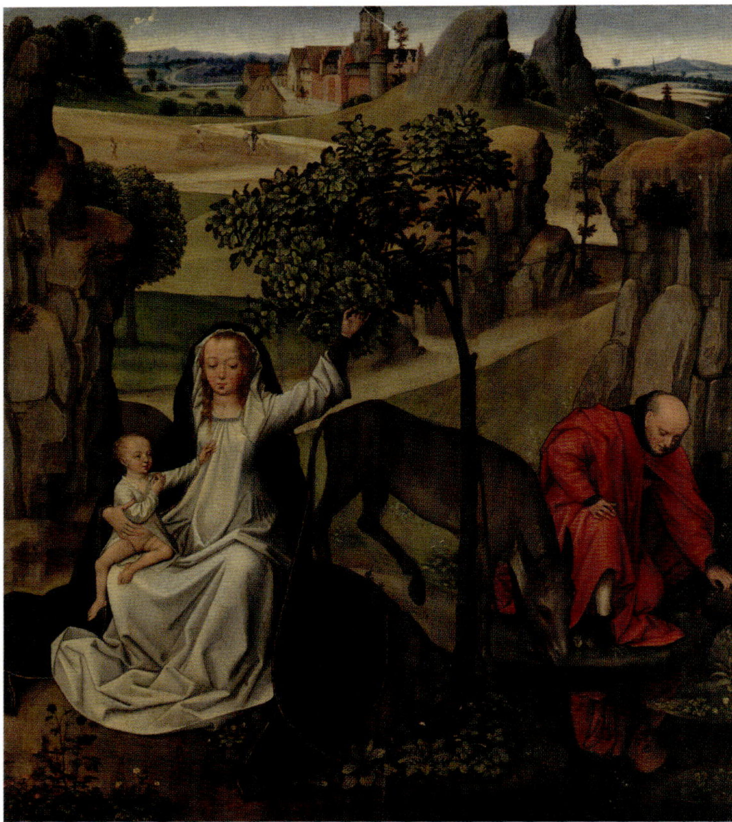

Burrell acquired the painting of the Virgin Annunciate thinking it to be by the illustrious Early Netherlandish painter Hans Memling. The dealer's brochure highlighted the presence of another related work, an Annunciation, on the London market. This information had been provided by the eminent specialist for Netherlandish art, Max Jakob Friedländer. Over a decade later Burrell was able to acquire it.

Today the works are believed not to be by the young Memling, but by another artist acquainted with his work, the so-called 'Master of the Prado *Adoration of the Magi*'. Burrell's paintings are two of only six associated with this particular artist.

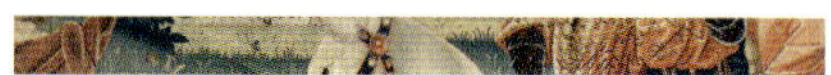

Tapestries

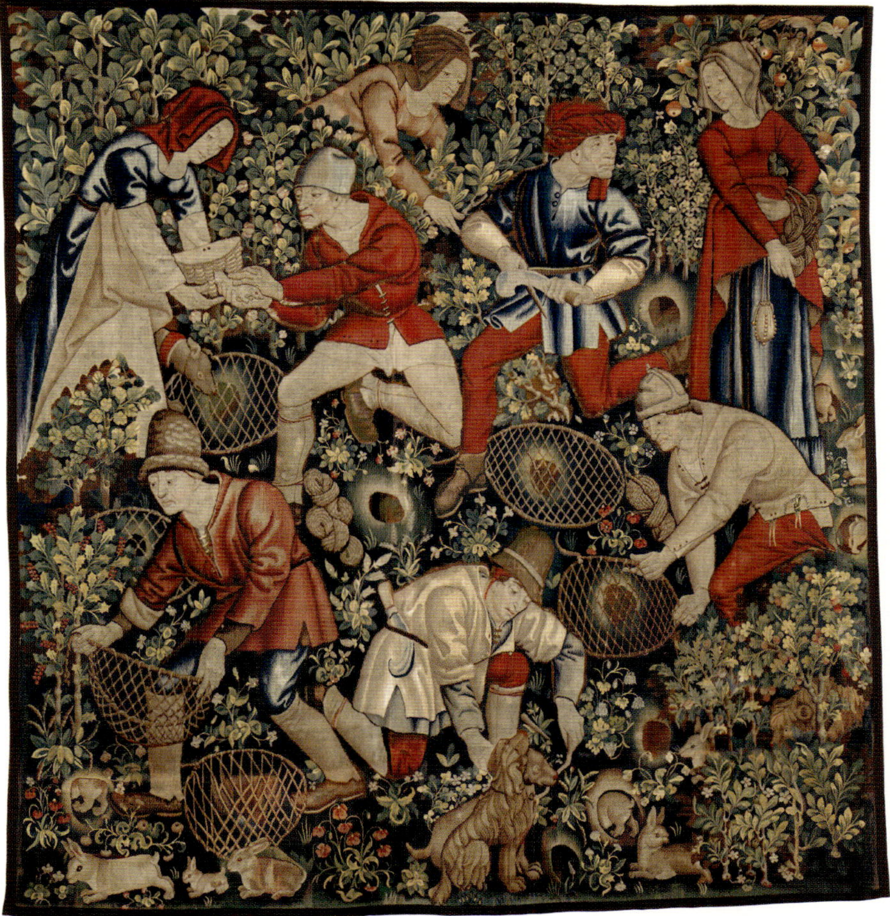

Peasants Preparing to Hunt Rabbits with Ferrets, about 1470–1490
Probably made in Brussels, the Southern Netherlands
Wool and silk, 3230 x 3000mm
46.56

The technical brilliance of the tapestry depicting *Peasants Preparing to Hunt Rabbits with Ferrets* places it among the finest products of medieval woven art. It demonstrates a freedom of treatment that is almost painterly in the rendering of foliage, fur and fabric, while the modelling of the figures is so masterly that it was once considered to be from a design by Rogier van der Weyden. The closely observed details of the peasants' costumes, however, provide a clue to the dating of the tapestry that puts it later than Van der Weyden's period of activity. It shows peasants busily preparing for the hunt by sharpening staves, arranging nets over rabbit holes and restraining dogs on leashes while a ferret is gently released from its basket. Aside from its artistic value, it is a pictorial document of the stages of the medieval hunt. Two related tapestries from the series illustrating the hunt and the picnic that follows are held by the Fine Arts Museums of San Francisco and the Louvre, Paris.

The Pursuit of Fidelity, about 1480–1490
Made in Alsace
Wool, silk, linen and metal threads, 800 x 880 x 5mm
46.28

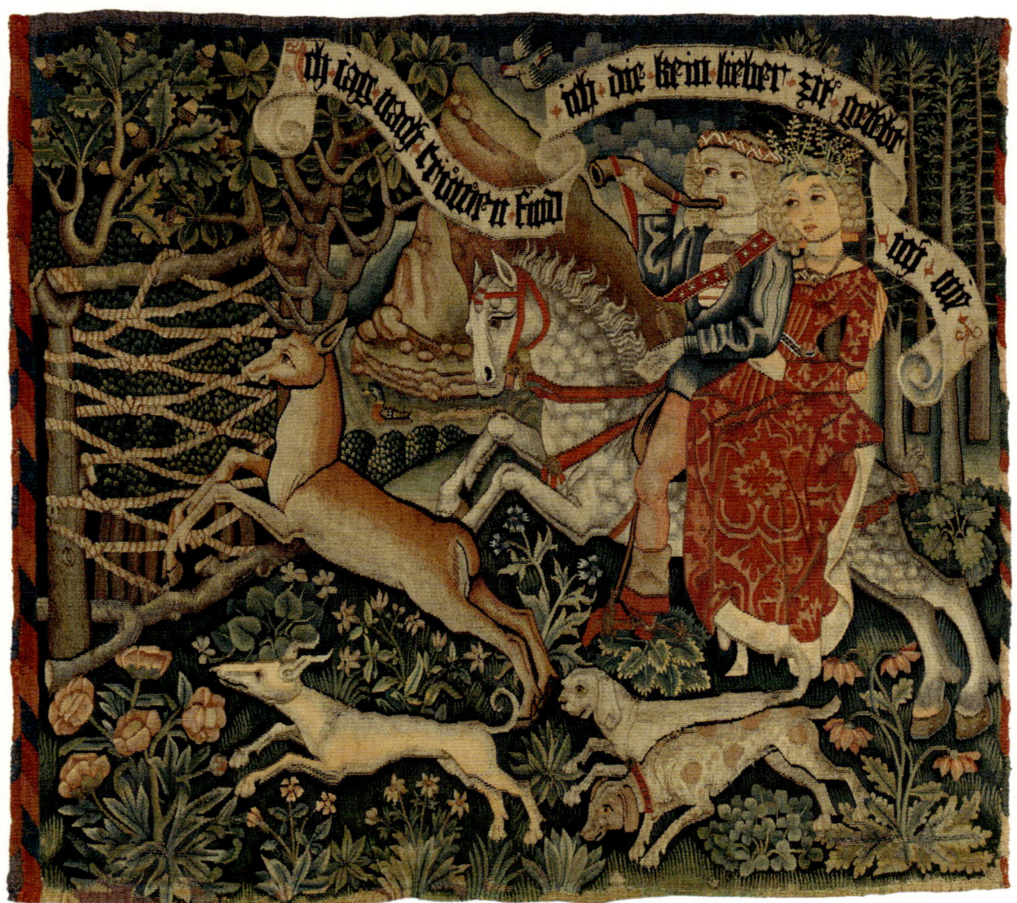

This joyful tapestry depicts a couple riding through the forest on a grey mare in pursuit of a lithe stag. The German text on a fluttering banner explains the meaning of the scene. It translates as: 'I hunt for fidelity; if this I find, I ask for nothing more'. Hunting scenes like this were popular in the late Middle Ages, serving as allegories of the romantic quest for true love.

Burrell positioned this tapestry and the tapestry of David and Bathsheba on either side of the bed in the Number One guest bedroom at Hutton Castle. The two are thematically linked and also stylistically similar. They belong to a body of tapestries attributed to workshops in Strasbourg, which, in the fifteenth century, was an important centre for the weaving of small-scale tapestries dedicated to secular and biblical scenes.

David and Bathsheba, about 1480
Made in Alsace
Wool, linen, silk and metal threads, 945 x 1074 x 17mm framed
46.27

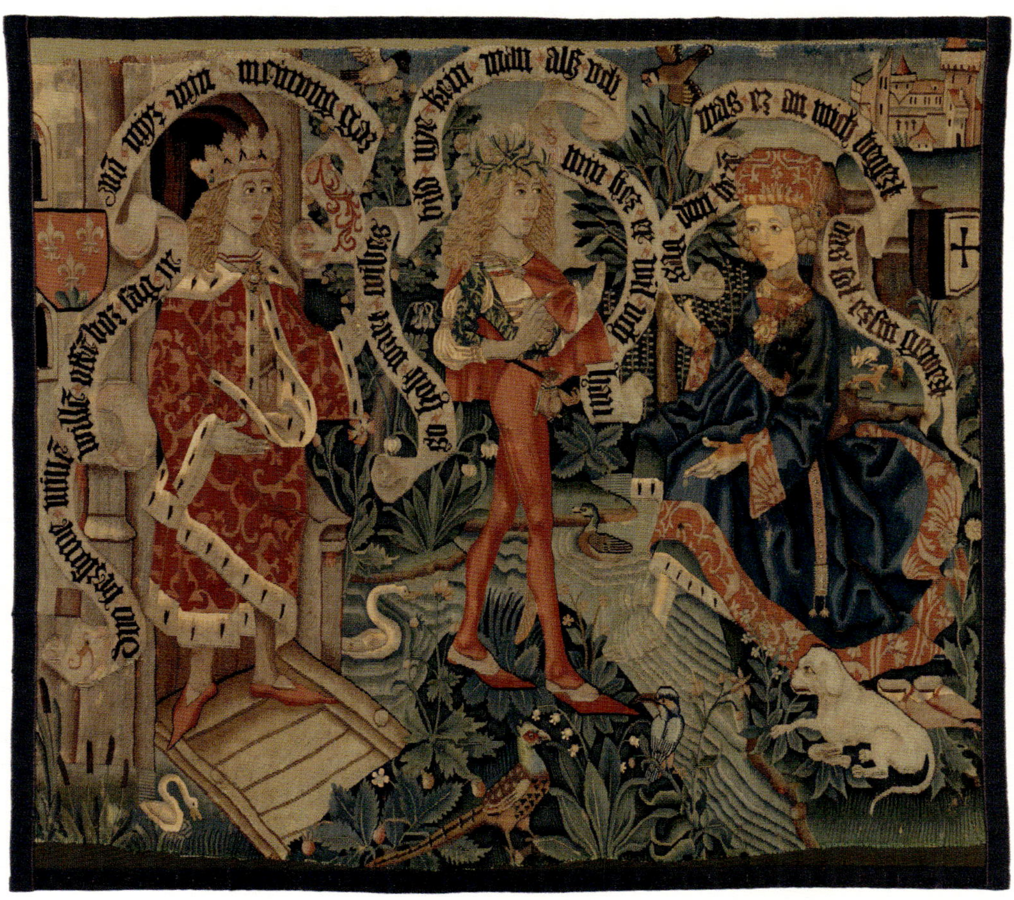

The work was commissioned by Heinrich Ingold, a wealthy Strasbourg merchant, and his wife, Clara Gerbott. Their family coats of arms flank the scene. This shows three figures dressed in the fashion of the 1480s: King David, on the left, Bathsheba on the right, and a messenger in the middle. The biblical Book of Samuel (II.2–5) tells how having seen Bathsheba bathing, David bade his servant approach her. His words to him (in German) are captured in a decorative scroll – 'Reveal to her my will; tell her of my intention'. The messenger's words to Bathsheba are captured similarly: 'There never was a man so in love as my master; he wants to possess you'. She responds: 'Tell your master, what he wishes from me shall be granted'. The subject, emphasizing male desire and female compliance, tells of marital duties. It has been suggested that it may have been intended to adorn the Ingold-Gerbott home.

***St Anne with the Virgin Mary and Christ Child,
and Four Saints,*** about 1480–1490
Made in the Middle Rhine Region, Germany
Wool, silk and metal threads, 770 x 1850mm
46.16

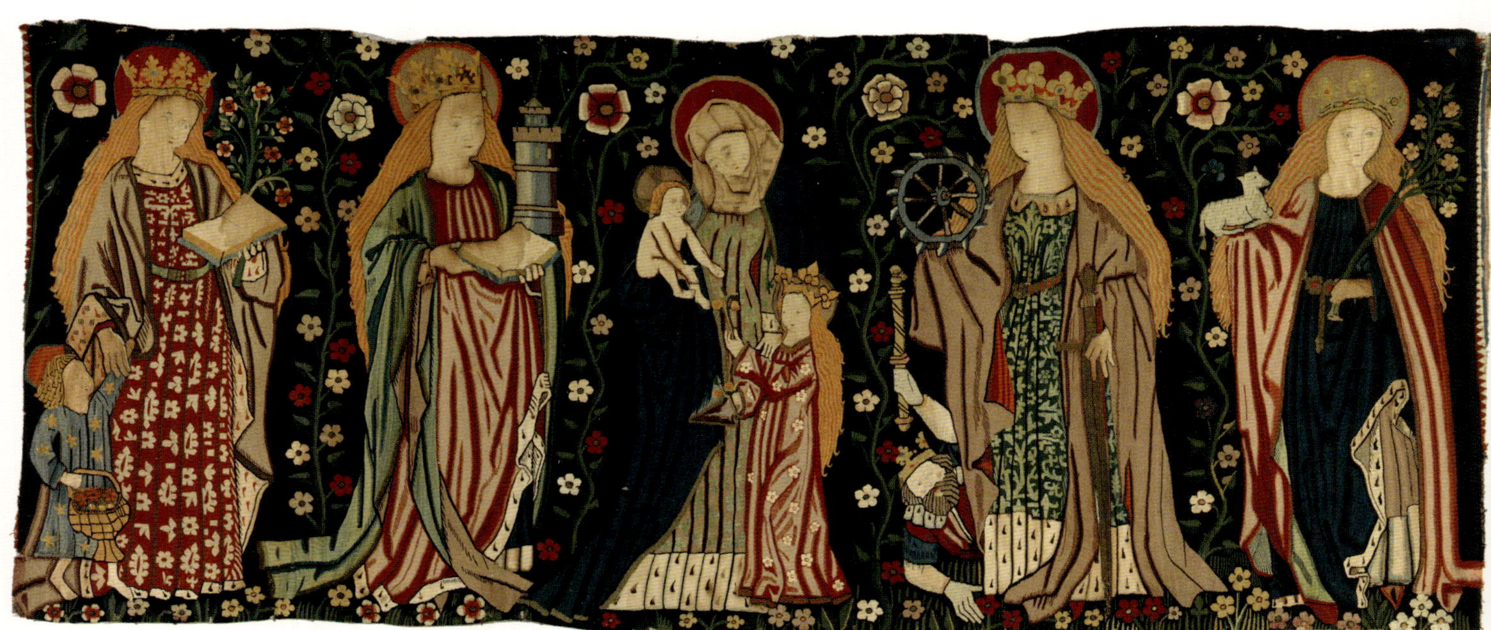

The dimensions of this small tapestry suggest that it perhaps originally served as an altar frontal. It represents five of the most significant female saints of the medieval period. In the centre is St Anne, the mother of the Virgin Mary, shown with her young daughter and the infant Christ. To either side are (from left to right) St Dorothy with a basket of flowers and a child; St Barbara with a tower; St Catherine with a wheel trampling the Emperor Maxentius underfoot; and St Agnes with a lamb. Contemporary prints are the most likely source for this composition. Such images of female virgin saints would have served to inspire cloistered women, and are known to have been commissioned by convents. This example is believed to have come from the Convent of Marienburg, near Boppard am Rhein, Germany.

Fight Between a Falcon and a Heron, about 1525
Made in Paris, France
Wool and silk, 3218 x 3140mm
46.60

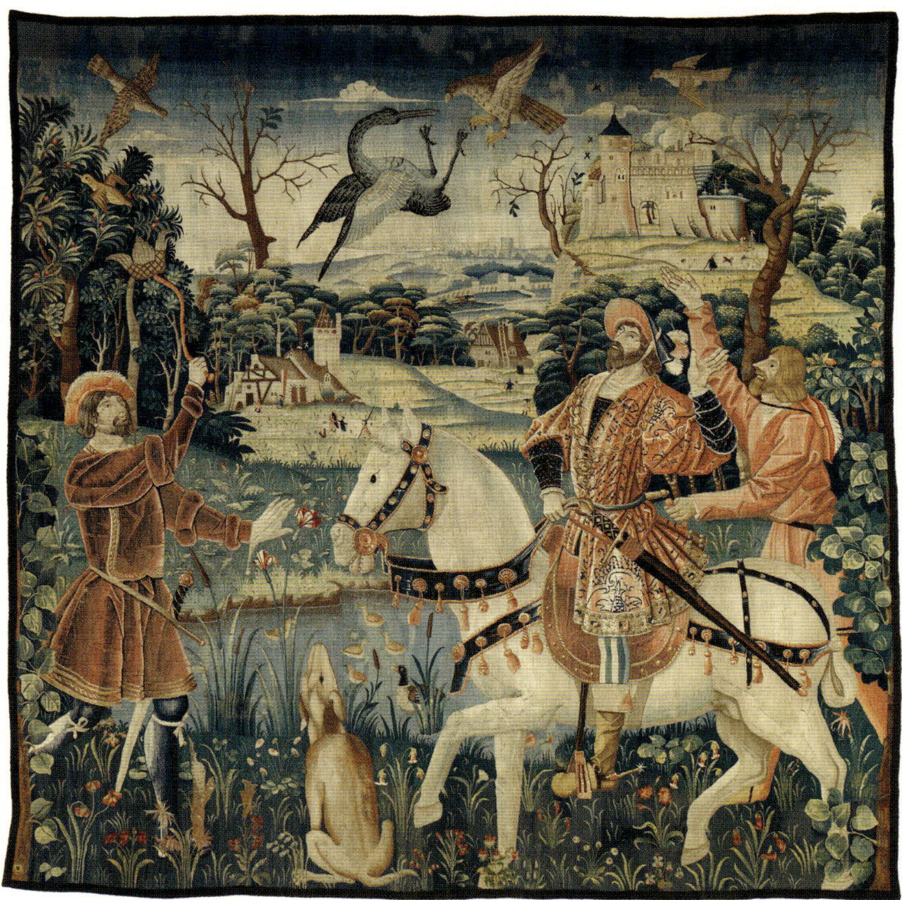

At the heart of this tapestry a heron and a falcon battle it out, both with primed talons and wide-open beaks uttering cries of attack and fear. On the left is the huntsman, who has loosed the falcon. On the right, a mounted noble and a page gesture upwards, observing the action above. Even their hound is entranced, his muzzle pointing arrow-like to the events in the sky, and to the comparatively peaceful receding landscape behind.

Burrell never found space for it at Hutton Castle. Instead he lent it almost immediately to Christ Church College, Oxford, where it remained until 1954. During his lifetime Burrell was a generous lender of his collection. His tapestries were seen in museums in Barnard Castle, Cambridge, Ipswich, Leicester, London, Luton, Newcastle, Perth, Oxford and Torquay as well as at Chichester, Durham, Ely, Salisbury and Winchester Cathedrals.

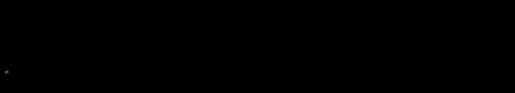

Stained Glass

Abraham Prepares to Sacrifice Isaac, around 1270
Made in Strasbourg, France
Clear, coloured and painted glass, lead, 465 x 485 x 10mm
Possibly from the Dominican Church, or the Church of St Thomas at Strasbourg
45.488

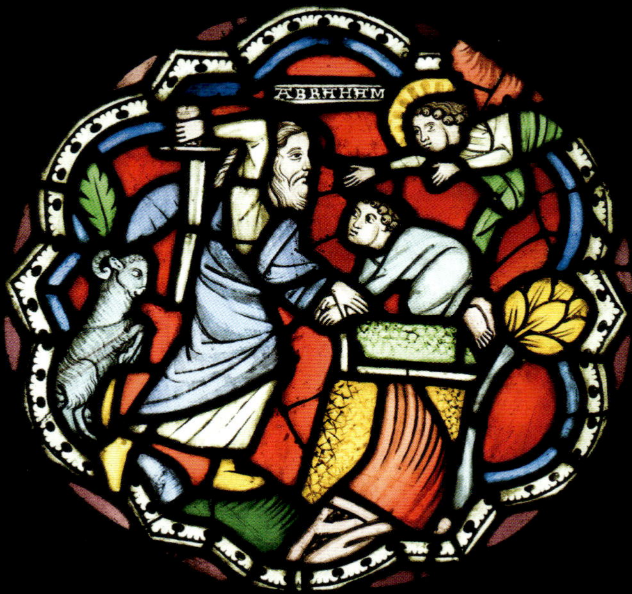

The Miracle at Cana, around 1255–1265
Probably made by the St John the Baptist atelier, Clermont-Ferrand, France
Clear, coloured and painted glass, lead, 520 x 620 x 10mm
45.366a-c

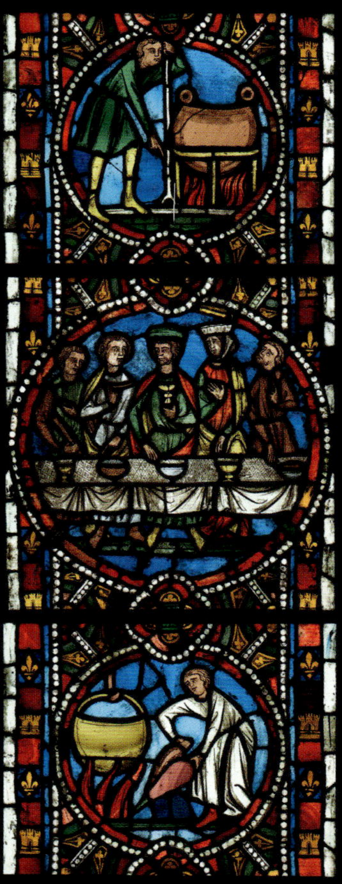

God asked Abraham to offer his son as a proof of his love for him. Here we see Abraham swinging the sword back, ready to strike the blow which will kill Isaac. The angel has appeared above them, calling a halt to the sacrifice. Behind Abraham is the ram which will take his son's place. This small medallion is now believed to have been removed from a church in Strasbourg in 1775, but at the time of its acquisition nothing was known about its history. When introducing Burrell to it in March 1939, Wilfred Drake accompanied its photograph with a copy of CH Sherrill's *Stained Glass Tours in Germany, Austria and the Rhineland* (1927) illustrating part of a window in Germany to give a flavour of its possible original appearance.

This set of three panels shows two cooks preparing for the feast in the middle medallion. At its centre, we see five figures alongside a table, one holding a wine cup, while the others look on and gesture in amazement. The transformation of water into wine at a marriage in Cana is the first miracle attributed to Jesus, according to the Gospel of John.

The window is now thought to have been removed from the Cathedral at Clermont-Ferrand, probably around the time of the restoration of the glass there between 1913 and 1922. Burrell himself acquired it from the collection of William Randolph Hearst in 1939.

**A *Priest Saint, possibly St Rimbert, and a Bishop Saint,
possibly St Nicholas of Myra or St Maternianus of Reims,***
Late 1200s–early 1300s
Clear, coloured and painted glass, lead, 1050 x 440 x 10mm each
Removed from the church of St Materniani and St Nicolai, Bücken
an der Weser, Lower Saxony, Northwestern Germany before 1914
46.28

Beatrix of Valkenburg, about 1293, and later
Probably from the church of the Greyfriars, Norwich, England
Made in Norwich, East Anglia, England
Coloured and painted glass, lead, 595 x 260 x 10mm
45.2

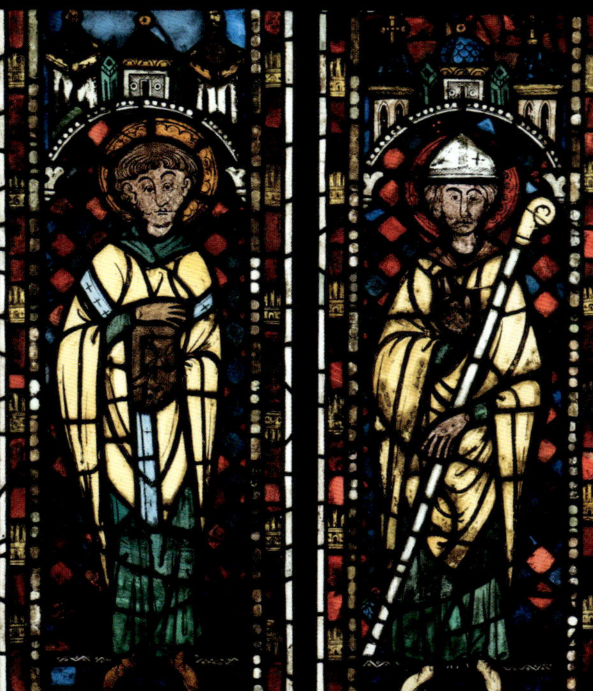

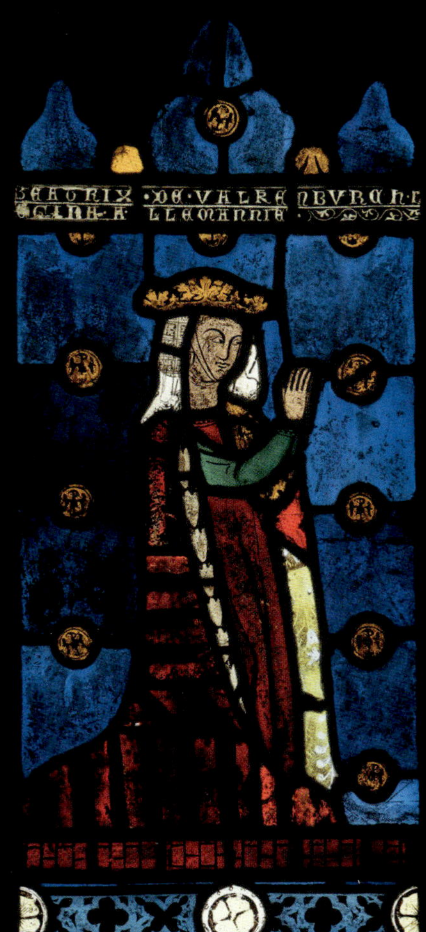

Like enormous leaded jigsaws, windows could be
dismantled and rebuilt to create new compositions.
This is what happened to Burrell's stained glass
panels depicting a Priest Saint and a Bishop Saint.
The two panels stood at the heart of a tall two-
light lancet window but the abstract ornament
surrounding the pair is suspiciously different. A
photograph of 1914 shows the three-quarter length
figures placed within a roundel. The panels appear
to have been enlarged sometime between 1914 and
their sale to Burrell from William Randolph Hearst's
collection in 1939. Wilfred Drake made Burrell aware
of this, pointing out that Burrell himself owned the
1914 book in which the image was published.

Not long after buying Hutton Castle, Burrell acquired
this stained glass panel depicting Beatrix van
Valkenburg (d.1277), the third wife of Richard of
Cornwall, King of the Romans. Recent research has
shown that this panel did not originate in the Church
of the Minorites in Oxford, as has long been thought,
but is instead probably from the Franciscan Church
in Norwich. Evidence suggests that it was paid for by
Beatrix's nephew King Edward I about 20 years after
her death.

Six windows showing the Life of Jesus Christ and the Virgin Mary, 1444
Made in the Upper Rhine Region, Germany
Clear, coloured and painted glass, lead, 2600 x 2300 x 10mm

45.485
Removed from the Carmelite Church of Boppard-am-Rhein. Showing Christ before Pilate and
The Agony in the Garden (left), the Annunciation, the Nativity (centre), the Resurrection of
Christ and Christ appearing to Peter

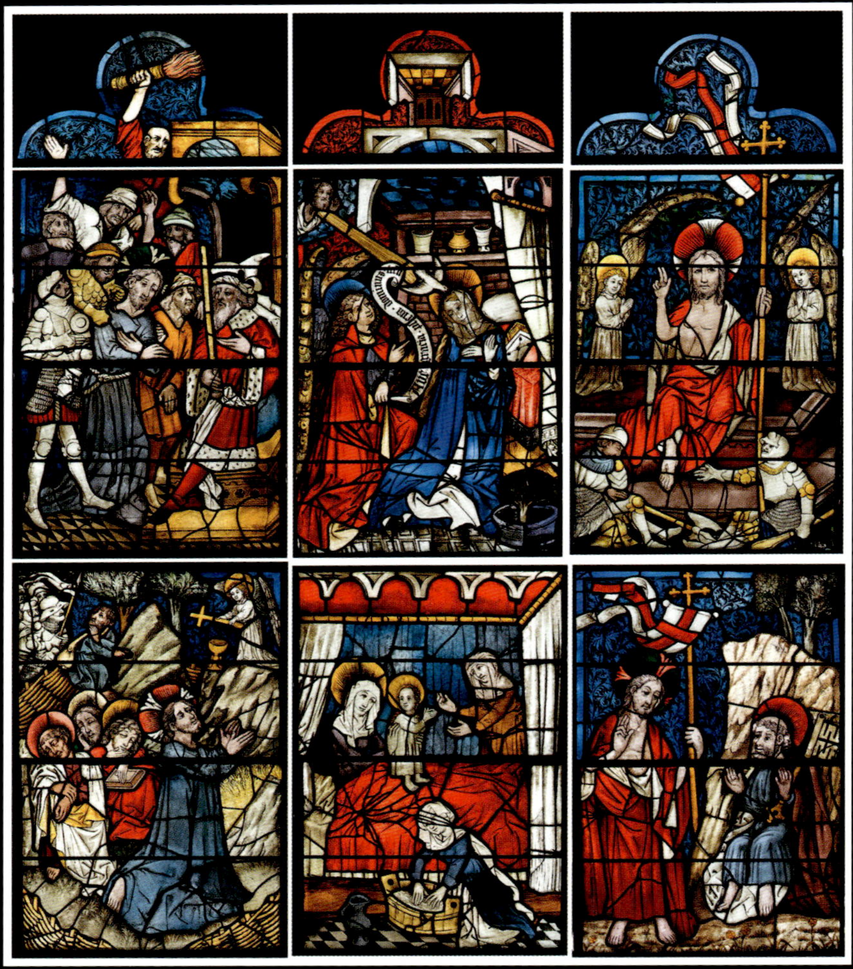

These panels are from the German town of Boppard-am-Rhein. The region's religious institutions suffered under the Napoleonic invasions and were secularized at the beginning of the 19th century. These windows were purchased whilst still in place in the north nave of Boppard's Carmelite Church, and subsequently removed in 1818 by a German count who hoped to use them in the decoration of his own home.

When this did not happen, his heir sold them onwards to the famous Parisian dealer Friedrich Spitzer. This caused a scandal in Germany, where the works were considered national treasures. The auction of Spitzer's collection after his death in 1887 was literally the sale of the century. These panels were acquired by the American millionaire Robert Goelet (d. 1899) who took them from Paris to the east coast of the United States. From there they travelled further westwards to California, where they entered the collection of William Randolph Hearst. With no actual window at Hutton capable of accommodating these, or the other windows he acquired from the church at Boppard, Burrell was able to enjoy these masterpieces of German glassmaking only on rare occasions.

Princess Cecily, about 1482–1487
Made in England
White, coloured, stained and painted glass, lead, 400 x 305mm
45.75

Princess Cecily of York (1469–1507) was the daughter of Edward IV and Elizabeth Woodville. This highly prized stained-glass panel depicting the princess originally formed part of the Royal window in the north-west transept of Canterbury Cathedral, removed in 1789. Wilfred Drake, the dealer who sold the panel to Burrell, suggested installing it close to that representing Beatrix van Valkenburg to comprise: 'a pair of English Royal portraits of different periods, …each of them a fine example and full of romantic interest.'

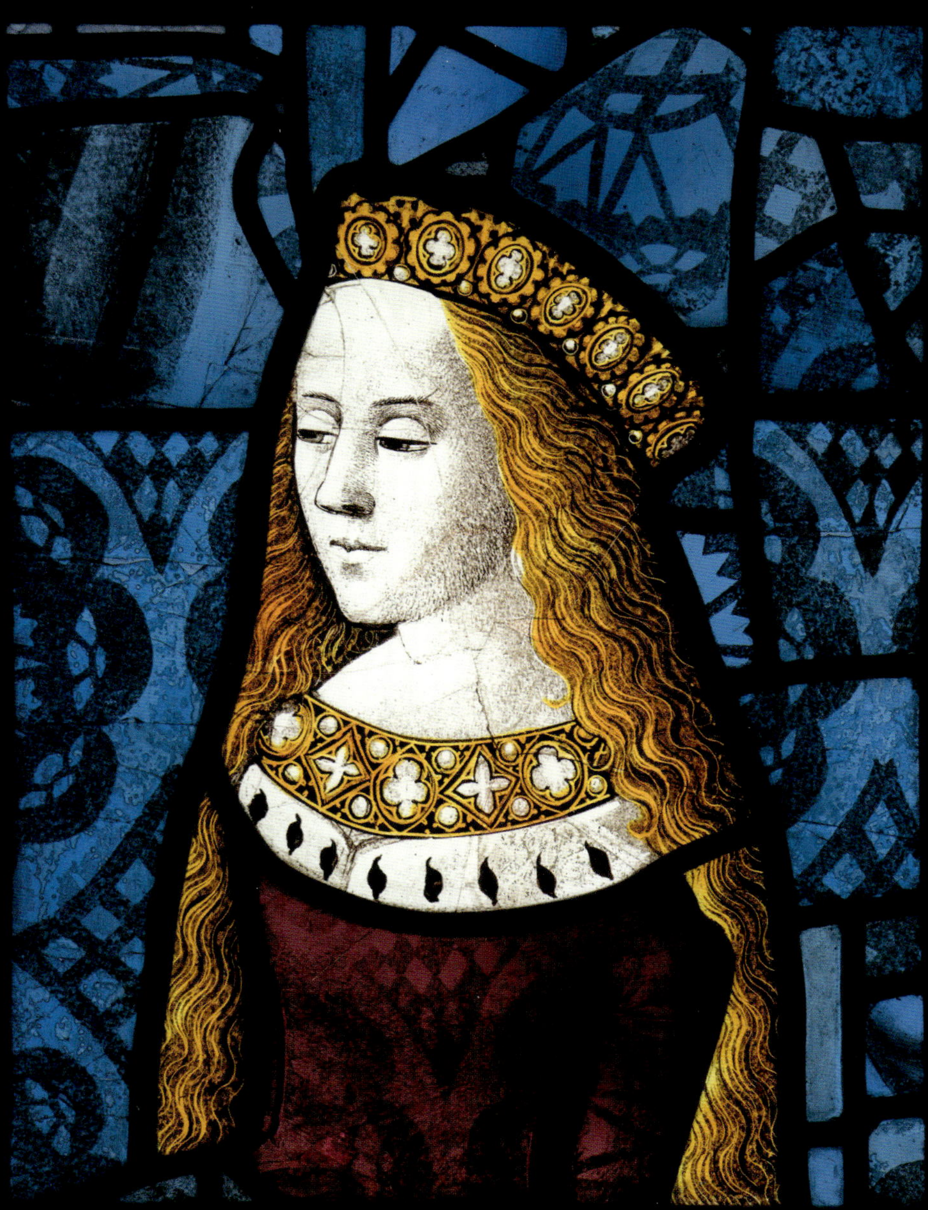

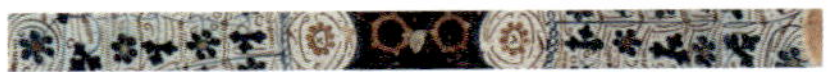

Ceramics

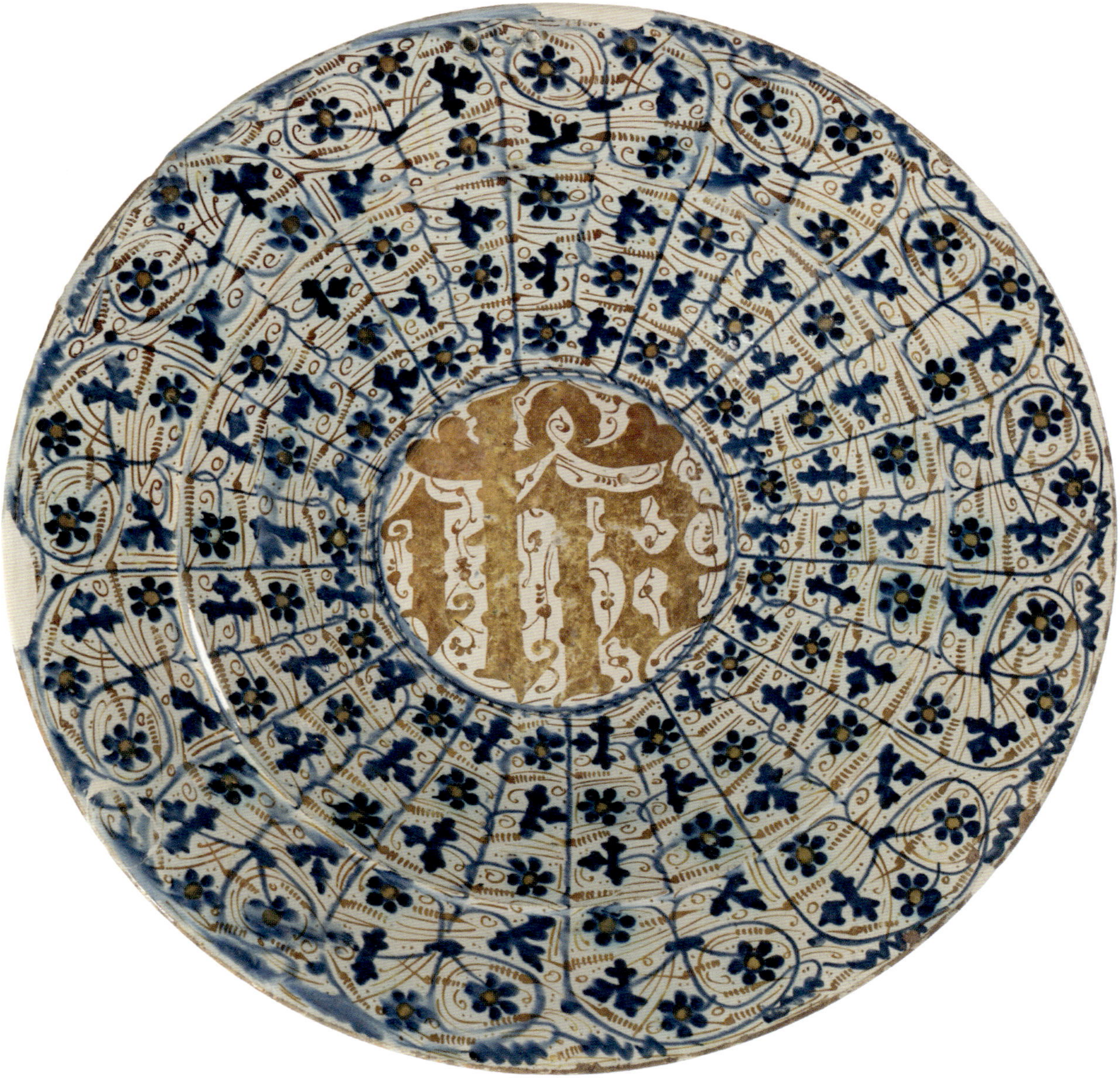

Dish with 'IHS' symbol of St Bernardino of Siena, 1430–1470
Made in Manises, Valencia, Spain
Tin-glazed earthenware, lustre decoration, 442 x 445 x 80mm

40.32

Starting around 1300, the small Spanish village of Manises grew into an important centre for the production of lustred tin-glazed earthenware, known today as hispano-moresque wares. The potters making them employed techniques learnt much further south in Andalucia. Documentary sources show that these craftspeople were frequently practising Muslims, while the works themselves were to be acquired by Christian clients. Thanks to the proximity of the port town of Valencia, these goods easily travelled further afield, not least to Italy, where many wealthy families commissioned lustrewares painted with their coats of arms, such as the dish with the shield of the Tondi family surrounded by stylized flowers and foliage.

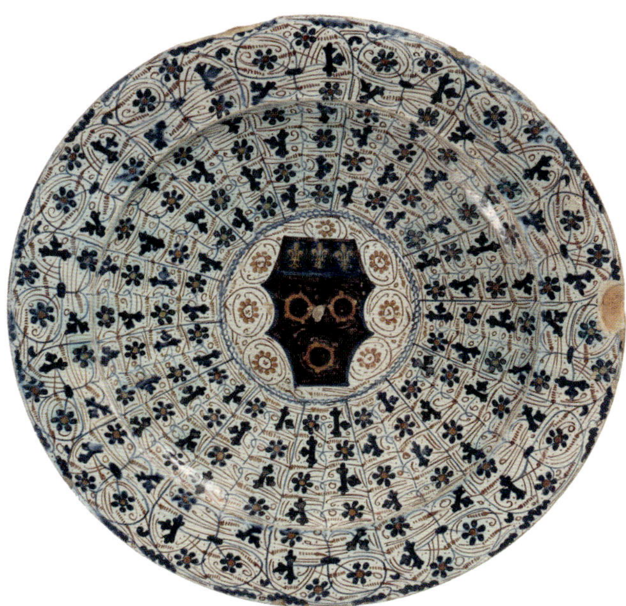

Dish with the shield of the Tondi family from Siena, Tuscany, about 1430–1470
Made in Manises, Valencia, Spain
Tin-glazed earthenware, lustre decoration, 451 x 449 x 21mm
40.25

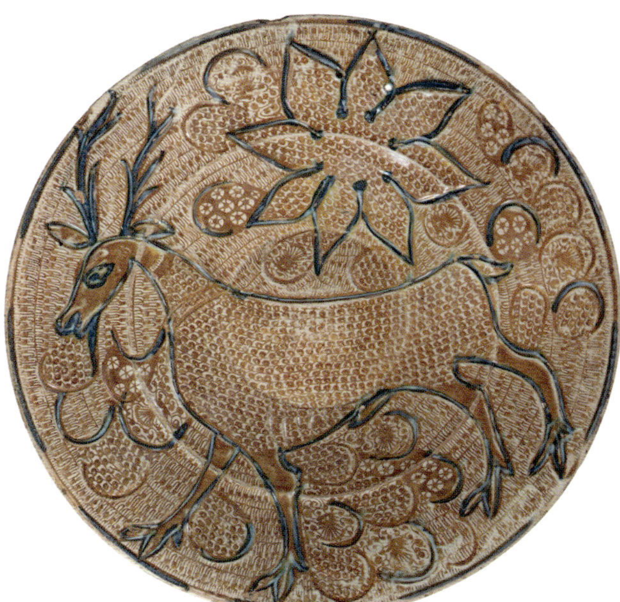

Dish decorated with a deer and 8-petalled flower, about 1500–1550
Made in Manises, Valencia, Spain
Tin-glazed earthenware, lustre decoration, 481 x 481 x 71mm
40.24

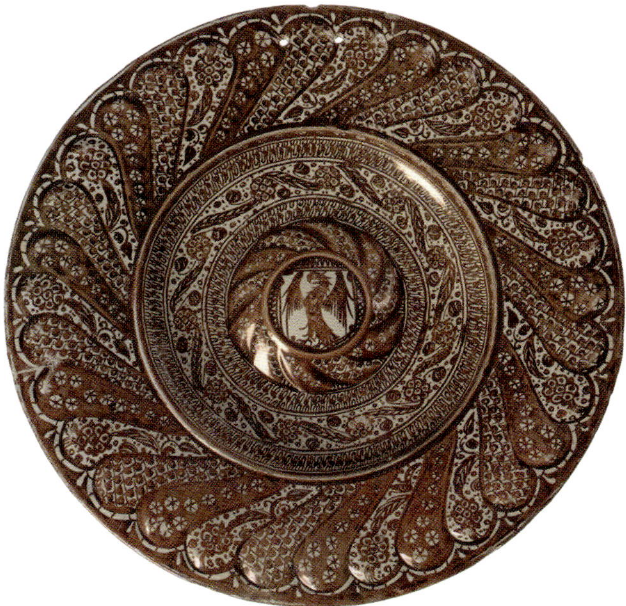

Dish with eagle shield, known as the 'Feversham Dish', about 1500–1550
Made in Manises, Valencia, Spain
Tin-glazed earthenware, lustre decoration, 481 x 481 x 65mm
40.27

ACKNOWLEDGEMENTS

Grateful thanks are extended to Rachel King, the project curator for this exhibition, and to Rosemary Watt, Rebecca Quinton and Claire Blakey for their insight and advice. Susan Pacitti has skilfully choreographed the various stages of this publication, which has been enhanced by Iona Shepherd's photography, while the exhibition's elegant design is due to the inspired touch of Jacqui Duffus. Glasgow Museums' Conservation team's care for the objects and advice on their display, and the Logistics team's build and lighting of the exhibition, are also gratefully acknowledged.

James Robinson
DIRECTOR
Burrell Renaissance

ISBN 978 1 908638 31 1

To find out more about the Burrell Collection Renaissance Project, visit www.glasgowlife.org.uk/museums/venues/the-burrell-collection

Design : Alasdair Robertson, StudioSVN

Printed in Scotland by Allander Print Limited